MY TUSCAN KITCHEN

MY TUSCAN KITCHEN

SEASONAL RECIPES FROM THE CASTELLO DI VICARELLO

AURORA BACCHESCHI BERTI

PHOTOGRAPHS BY
BETH EVANS

WRITTEN WITH
ANNE HANLEY

FOREWORD BY
JULIAN NICCOLINI

RIZZOLI
NEW YORK

New York Paris London Milan

First published in the United States of America in 2011
by Rizzoli International Publications, Inc.
300 Park Avenue South
New York, NY 10010
www.rizzoliusa.com

2011 2012 2013 2014 / 10 9 8 7 6 5 4 3 2 1
Designed by Mike Bone
Edited by Christopher Steighner
Printed in China
ISBN: 978-0-8478-3593-5
Library of Congress Control Number: 2010940961

CONTENTS

FOREWORD

LIKE A FAIRY tale castle, hidden in the forests of Tuscany's Maremma region, Castello di Vicarello is one of the world's most delicious destinations. A twelfth-century estate with romantic views of vineyards and olive groves, it is the dream home of Carlo and Aurora Baccheschi Berti, winemakers known for creating truly spectacular Super Tuscans and Maremma's most luxurious cuisine.

When we talk about food luxuries, some mistakenly think about wildly expensive ingredients and impossibly elaborate presentations. But that's not luxury. That's pretense. Delicious food is like a beautiful woman. She doesn't need a designer dress or a yoke of diamonds around her neck to seduce a crowd. On the contrary, her true beauty lies in her confidence, in simply being true to herself, because real beauty and genuine luxury is about honesty.

One of Italy's most natural chefs, Aurora is nothing if not passionate about culinary honesty, and the genius of her recipes lies in their confident simplicity. Like an artist, Aurora begins each dish with the freshest seasonal ingredients available. Of course she, like everyone else in these modern times, could find tomatoes in the winter or pumpkins in springtime, but that's not how Aurora sources her ingredients.

Aurora respects the romance of waking up on a beautiful morning and strolling through her garden in search of the produce that has reached its peek and is bursting with true flavor. Using the natural world as her culinary collaborator, she also picks wild herbs, forages for mushrooms, raises her own poultry, and even hunts game in Maremma's magical countryside.

What I love about her recipes is that Aurora also respects the true characteristics of each ingredient. She never uses fancy sauces, contrived cooking techniques, or acrobatic presentations. She has an unwavering respect for the nourishment pure foods provide and how we sensually consume them with our eyes, our mouths, our noses, and our sense of touch.

Like a fairy godmother with a magic wand, Aurora simply presents the ingredients in a way that unveils their true beauty and flavor. And while she has supreme respect for Italy's culinary traditions, Aurora is an innovator. She recognizes that every true cook can and should bring something personal to age-old recipes. It is that impulse to add a dash of love to each recipe that just may be her secret ingredient.

I hope you like these recipes as much as I do and as much as my guests at the Four Seasons Restaurant have. Not long ago, I hosted a dinner in the restaurant's Pool Room in honor of Carlo Baccheschi Berti's amazing wines. To make the party authentic, I asked Aurora for recipes that honestly reflect the Tuscany of my childhood. The results were nothing short of deliciously sublime.

Julian Niccolini
Managing Partner
The Four Seasons Restaurant

INTRODUCTION

I HAVE ALWAYS been passionate about cooking, but it wasn't until I left my home in northern Italy, grew tired of my foreign travels, and settled down in the coastal area of Tuscany called the Maremma that I truly learned to cook.

When I first stumbled across the Maremma during a holiday in Tuscany in the 1970s, no one had ever heard of this land of rolling hills and scattered farmhouses, where sea breezes blow through enchanted oak forests. The moment I laid eyes on the castle of Vicarello—then a crumbling ruin inhabited only by grazing Maremman cattle and a family of owls—I was in love: I knew I had to find a way to buy this ancient structure and breathe life back into it. Luckily, my husband, Carlo, supported me in my madness. Vicarello became the passion of our lives.

Though I bought Vicarello in 1980, it wasn't until 1993 that we decided to move to the Maremma permanently. With our three children in tow, we embarked upon ten years of painstaking restoration work to transform the dilapidated shell into what has become a unique guesthouse. It was a true labour of love. We faced innumerable challenges over the years, dealing with Italy's byzantine bureaucracy and unreliable workmen who would begin jobs then disappear without warning or explanation. But we persevered through good times and bad, and in the end we saw our visions become reality.

Here in the Maremma I discovered a whole new approach to cooking, where the honest flavors of locally produced ingredients lend even the simplest of traditional dishes an unexpected elegance. My Tuscan neighbors provided inspiration and practical advice, and none more so than the wonderful Olema Ginanneschi, mother of nine children and an extraordinary cook.

Olema's was one of the last of the tenant farming families to live in the castle before it was finally abandoned in the early 1950s; in fact, she was born here, in what is now one of our suites. We met her and her angel of a husband, Angiolino, in 1978 and for many years they worked for us.

Though they have now retired, they remain close to our hearts: our children still call her Nonna (Grandma) Olema. It was Olema who taught me the traditions and secrets of the Maremman kitchen, handing unwritten recipes down to me as local mothers do to their daughters. Olema showed me the secrets of Acqua Cotta (page 228), literally "cooked water" but one of the most delicious soups imaginable, and of Tortelli Maremmani (page 37), a light filled pasta that is a specialty of the area.

To make the pasta for the tortelli, she taught me how to make the dough (page 38): Using twenty eggs, she would make one immense sheet of pasta—large enough to cover my huge kitchen table. She never, however, measured or weighed a single ingredient. Very much in the same spirit, I hate to be a slave to the scales and the clock; I trust my instincts. The results may vary each time I make a dish, but—crucially—my imagination and inventiveness are constantly fired.

Naturally, my publisher felt that readers might appreciate a little more detail on weights, measures, and cooking times. I have struggled over this but the process has, I have to admit, been an education for me. After decades of guesswork, counting sage or basil leaves and measuring ingredients to the last ounce have taught me to appreciate precision too— sometimes! Though you can opt to follow my recipes to the letter, it would make me happy to think you were also taking them as jumping-off points for open-minded improvisation.

I LOVE COOKING in my great kitchen at Vicarello. For me it's a magician's cave, with its vintage 1957 Triplex stove and two glorious gas ovens. It is here that we prepare most of our dishes and give cooking courses to our guests. A friend once said that Vicarello's kitchen is its lobby, and it's true. This is where guests congregate, glass of wine in hand, to see what's cooking and to snack on Carlo's savory wild boar sausages. This makes perfect sense to us, as the kitchen really is where it all happens.

I divide my personal recipe collection by season and by course, as I have done in this book. This makes it easy for me to decide on a dish, or to mix and match to create new meals each day.

When I invent a new dish, I first prepare it for family and friends. With their feedback, I make adjustments and add it to my repertoire. But mostly I love to play with traditional recipes, simplifying to make them lighter and more modern. I love fresh ingredients, distinct flavors, and beautiful colors on the plate. Food should be a feast for the eyes as well!

This book contains mainly Maremman recipes, which I have been fortunate enough to be able to get down in writing. But I have also included some recipes from Sicily—another part of Italy I find endlessly inspiring—and from my native region of Lombardy.

AFTER MANY YEARS of welcoming guests to Castello di Vicarello, and building my repertoire of recipes, the idea of putting it all down in a book came almost by chance.

One day in summer 2007, Beth Evans, a brilliant British photographer, arrived at Vicarello to shoot the property for an article in *Condé Nast Traveller UK*. At lunch, under the pergola covered with *fragolino* grapes, eating eggplant parmigiana, Beth asked me if I had ever thought about writing a cookbook. I hadn't, but by the time we finished lunch, Beth had convinced me. Anne Hanley, a British garden designer and journalist living in Italy, was brought on board and became the patient translator of my recipes and voice of my memories.

Together over the next year, and following the seasons, we congregated in my kitchen to cook, photograph, and eat all of the dishes included in this book. We put on a few pounds, certainly, but we enjoyed ourselves in the process!

A FEW NOTES ON INGREDIENTS

IN ALL MY cooking I use fruit, vegetables, and meat that were produced either on our own land or on a farm—and preferably organic. In my opinion there is simply no comparison between the taste of this fresh, natural produce and the insipid flavors of industrially produced goods. Everyone, of course, is entitled to their own opinion about the health and ethical implications of natural-organic versus agro-industrial. But as far as flavor is concerned, the former wins hands down every time.

Bacon: Pancetta is at the base of many Italian recipes, but since it is not always available elsewhere, it can be replaced with bacon. Note, however, that while pancetta is not smoked, bacon is, which adds an extra element to the taste of any recipe. If you can obtain pancetta, therefore, use it instead. For all of these recipes, I use *pancetta stesa* or *pancetta rigatino*, which is shaped flat like slab bacon. Note this is different from *pancetta arrotolata*, the rolled type of pancetta found in many specialty shops.

Cheeses: If you can, it is worth sourcing the genuine, imported Italian article for recipes calling for Parmigiano-Reggiano, pecorino, or Grana Padano. If you have no reliable importer in your vicinity, always sustitute high-quality local equivalents. Do not use the bland, industrially produced hard Italian cheeses—the result will be very disappointing indeed.

Chili: Whenever a recipe calls for this, it is where I use *peperoncino piccante*, a fresh hot red chili pepper. You may substitute fresh Anaheim or cherry peppers, or dried red chili flakes, to taste.

Eggs: These are always medium size.

Herbs: When a recipe calls for 1 bunch of a fresh herb, this means approximately 1 ounce.

Olive oil: I use exclusively extra virgin olive oil, from our own olive trees. Of course, few people are lucky enough to be able to use their own produce like this, but I strongly recommend splurging on a high-quality oil; it will make all the difference.

Salt: I prefer using sea salt.

Semolina flour: Semolina flour has a texture coarser than all-purpose flour. When used to make pasta, semolina allows the sauce to cling to the surface better. It also adds a lovely golden color. Especially for pasta, do seek out semolina flour (which is sometimes called durum flour). You may need to order it online.

THE ITALIAN MEAL

THE CLASSIC, FULL Italian meal begins with an *antipasto* (starter), then continues with a *primo* (first course), which generally consists of soup, risotto, or pasta. You would then expect to be served a meat or fish *secondo* (main course), accompanied by a *contorno* (vegetable side dish). To follow, you would be served a *dolce* (dessert).

It's fairly rare, in this day and age, for anyone to eat one's way through so many courses, except on special occasions. At Vicarello, however, I prefer to serve very small helpings of a large number of dishes to give my guests the chance to sample as many local specialities as possible.

I have labelled each of my recipes according to the courses they would naturally belong to. But by varying the size of the serving, you could certainly turn many of the *antipasti* into *secondi*, or some *contorni* into starters. Vegetarians, in particular, will find a host of potential main courses hidden among the *antipasti* and the side dishes. I'd like to think that each user of this book will adapt my recipes to suit his or her own tastes and purposes.

Aurora Baccheschi Berti

LA PRIMAVERA

LA PRIMAVERA
SPRING

THE BUSY HOLIDAY season is approaching at Vicarello, and early spring is the time to make sure everything's ready for the arrival of warm weather and the first guests, around Easter. We just placed an order for crisp new linen napkins, and the huge new trays have finally arrived. The choice of trays was a difficult one: silver just didn't seem to go with the spirit of the place, so I had them made out of beautifully finished dark wood. Made on the premises, on the other hand, are the chewy caramels, wrapped in colored tissue paper, which guests find in their rooms on arrival. Their irresistible flavor comes from honey, which we collect from hives in our hunting reserve and then cook down for hours with equal quantities of cream and sugar.

In the vineyards, Carlo is beginning his annual—organic—battle against predators. New tracts planted over the winter have had to be ringed with strong wire fences to keep marauding boars away from the tender plants. Now is the time for the first treatment with bordeaux mixture (copper sulfate and lime) to ward off fungal diseases. Vineyard workers are busy spreading manure to ensure a vigorous crop.

The vibrant spring colors that fill the fields all around the castle have found their way inside too, in great bunches of spring flowers: the brilliant yellow of the ubiquitous *Sinapis arvensis*—charlock—stands out. I fill all the rooms with blossoms—starting with the kitchen, which is the heart of my house. To best display their beauty, I have amassed a collection of big, old terra cotta vases. I buy them wherever I can find them, even if they are a little broken. The woods and borders around the castle now also yield one of spring's greatest treats: tiny spears of strongly flavored wild asparagus, poking up between their frondy, scratchy foliage. Hunting for them becomes a game in which I invite guests—and my sons—to participate. Whoever collects the most asparagus wins! We return to the castle and cook enormous omelettes with our spoils.

LA PRIMAVERA
SPRING

IN THE GARDEN

THE *ORTO* (GARDEN) is already bursting with life, and neat rows of peas, spinach, fava beans, and onions are almost ready for picking. Our palates are lightening and we yearn for the first vegetables, to be prepared raw or lightly cooked. Peas and fava beans are early treats in these parts, the latter eaten mostly raw, freshly picked and podded, in salads or simply accompanied by sharp pecorino cheese. It won't be long until the first waxy new potatoes are ready to be dug up. But until then, digging focuses mainly on the jungle of weeds, brought forth in abundance by the spring warmth after the winter rain.

Once per month from now until August we plant the arugula and many other kinds of lettuce, in order to have a constant, steady crop. The herbs go in the ground too, and now also is the time I order flower seeds to plant later in summer. Among my favorites: cosmos, aquilegia, calendula, and sunflowers. And I always seem to find a little more space for roses.

Three long rows of artichoke plants are full of the small round heads, ready for eating raw or cooking. Later on in the season, when the novelty of so many *carciofi* has worn off, I will begin bottling them: using only the tiny tender late artichokes, I remove the tough outer leaves and cut off the spiny tips of the leaves that remain; these go in a saucepan with a mixture of two parts water, one part wine, and one part wine vinegar, along with peppercorns, bay, sage, and chili. Once it's boiling, I pop the artichokes in to cook for a couple of minutes. Drained, the artichokes are left standing, head down, on paper towels for twenty-four hours, then placed—again, head down—in glass jars and covered with olive oil, which will preserve them for months.

Spring is a sequence of fruits—strawberries, cherries, then raspberries—which ripen in abundance and require swift processing. Any that aren't eaten immediately I turn into jam: I prefer a minimal amount of sugar (about 1 cup to every 2 pounds of fruit) in order to let the flavors of the fruit shine through. The fruit, chopped if necessary, is boiled with the sugar for about half an hour, until a little of the mixture dribbled on a saucer doesn't run. Then I pour it into sterilized jars, tighten the lids, and boil the jars in a pot for 35 minutes. These jams we keep in the pantry for months, to brighten up the dark days of winter.

EASTER TRADITIONS

EASTER IN RURAL Tuscany is keenly felt, and closely tied to the natural rhythm of the place. On Palm Sunday, we cut olive branches from the trees and present them at church to be blessed. Hung up on the wall back in our kitchen, the branches will protect our home for the year. Then for Easter Sunday, we fill a basket with colored hard-boiled eggs and a Tuscan salami. This we take to be placed on the church altar, which is filled with similar baskets prepared by other local families. After the priest blesses all the baskets, we bring ours back home and use the contents as an antipasto to start our Easter lunch. It is followed by spring tastes such as Fava Bean and Artichoke Salad (page 22), Tortelli (page 38), Lamb Baked in Milk (page 46), and Zuccotto (page 66) and Brioche Dove (page 68) for dessert.

MAMME (MAMMOLE) RIPIENE
STUFFED ARTICHOKES

Serves four

4 *romanesco* artichokes

¼ cup breadcrumbs

3 slices pancetta, ½ inch thick, minced

Leaves from 1 bunch parsley, minced

2 cloves garlic, minced

1 chili, minced

1 tablespoon Aromatic Salt (page 46)

6 tablespoons extra virgin olive oil

Pork fatback (or bacon rind), for lining the dish

Preheat the oven to 350°F.

Remove the stalks from the artichokes, peel off the stringy outside layer, and finely chop the stalks. Place them in a bowl and add the breadcrumbs, bacon, parsley, garlic, chili, salt, and 4 tablespoons of the olive oil.

Remove the chokes from the artichoke heads. Wash the heads under running water, drain them, and open them up gently, spreading the "petals." Place the artichoke stalk mixture carefully between the petals. Rotate the heads gently between your hands to close the petals.

Stand the artichokes upright in an ovenproof dish with a piece of fatback underneath each: the fat will add flavor to the artichokes and keep them from sticking. Drizzle the artichokes with the remaining 2 tablespoons olive oil. Bake for 1½ hours, until the artichokes are slightly browned and tender.

This ancient Tuscan recipe is best made with spherical romanesco *globe artichokes, which look rather like a large, green peony bud; they're commonly known as* mamme *or* mammole. *The recipe was handed down by the grandmother of my truly Tuscan husband, Carlo. The baked artichokes are excellent cold and will keep for several days in the refrigerator.*

ASPARAGI SALTATI
ASPARAGUS WITH PANCETTA

Serves four

2 slices pancetta, minced

2 eggs

1¾ pounds asparagus, trimmed

3 tablespoons extra virgin olive oil

Salt

Juice of ½ lemon

Country-style bread for serving

Place the pancetta in a skillet over medium-high heat and toss until it is crisp.

Boil the eggs in a small pot of water for 7 minutes, drain and cool, then peel and finely chop them.

Place the asparagus in a skillet and drizzle the oil over it. Place over medium heat and season with salt. Sauté for about 4 minutes, turning the spears constantly until they are tender.

Place the asparagus on a serving dish and dress with the lemon juice to taste (2 teaspoons should be about right). Sprinkle with the pancetta and egg, and serve with slices of toasted country-style bread.

Try to find thinner stalks of asparagus and those with purplish tips; I find they are more flavorful and are certainly the best for this recipe.

INSALATA DI FAVE FRESCHE, CARCIOFI, PECORINO E NOCI
FAVA BEAN AND ARTICHOKE SALAD

Serves six

4 pounds fava beans

6 baby artichokes

Lemon juice

2 ounces sharp pecorino, thinly sliced

½ cup walnuts

¼ cup extra virgin olive oil

Salt and freshly ground black pepper

Leaves from 1 bunch marjoram, minced

Shell the fava beans, then remove the waxy outer coat from each of them.

Wash the artichokes and discard the tough outer leaves. Halve the artichokes and thinly slice. Plunge the slices into a bowl of water with lemon juice in it to keep them from turning brown. Drain and dry the slices and place them in a salad bowl with the pecorino, fava beans, and walnuts.

Dress with the oil, season with salt and pepper, and sprinkle with the marjoram leaves.

For Tuscans, fava beans are part of the arrival of spring; they are rarely cooked, mostly eaten raw. You'll find great heaps of them on dining tables, ready to be podded and peeled, and eaten with delicious aged pecorino cheese. Peeling the individual beans is time-consuming: it's easier if you first drop them into boiling water for 30 seconds.

RAVEGGIOLO
FRESH CHEESE

Yields about one and one-half cups

1½ quarts fresh cow's or goat's milk

⅓ teaspoon liquid rennet mixed with 1 tablespoon water

Salt and freshly ground black pepper

Extra virgin olive oil

In a large saucepan, heat the milk just until it is warm to the touch, 95°F, then remove it from the heat and add the rennet.

Let stand for 2 hours. Skim off the curds with a large strainer lined with cheesecloth. Tie the corners of the cheesecloth and hang it for 1 hour to allow excess milk to drip off. If you like, you can pack the cheese into a lightly greased decorative mold, and then turn it out onto a plate (see top of photo on page 23).

Season with salt and pepper, drizzle with olive oil, and serve.

This is excellent served with fresh fava beans in spring or with microgreens in any season. Drizzled with honey, it also makes a tasty dessert. Making fresh cheese is so very simple, yet the rich final product is always an unexpected delight. You can buy rennet from any number of online cheesemakers' supply shops.

ANTIPASTO/SECONDO

TORTA DI PORRI
LEEK FLAN

Serves four to six

For the pastry

1 cup all-purpose flour

1 cup semolina flour

2 tablespoons extra virgin olive oil

Leaves from 1 bunch each chives, thyme, and parsley, minced

½ teaspoon salt

For the filling

6 large leeks

3 tablespoons extra virgin olive oil

1 clove garlic, unpeeled

1 chili, minced

Salt and freshly ground black pepper

½ cup grated aged pecorino

In a food processor, combine the two flours, the oil, herbs, and salt. Turn the machine on, gradually add about ⅓ cup of water, and process until a soft ball of pastry forms. Wrap it in plastic wrap and refrigerate for 1 hour.

Preheat the oven to 350°F and grease an 11-inch baking dish.

Trim and discard the toughest green ends from the leeks. Wash the rest carefully under running water and cut into 2-inch lengths.

Crush the garlic clove with the flat blade of a knife and place it in a skillet along with the oil and the chili. Place over medium heat. When the oil is hot, add the leeks, season with salt and pepper, and stir with a wooden spoon until softened; if the leeks start to dry out, add a ladle of water.

Discard the garlic, place the leeks in a bowl, and adjust the seasoning if necessary.

Roll out the pastry to a ⅛-inch thickness and line the prepared baking dish with it, leaving some pastry hanging over the side of the dish. Spoon the leeks over the pastry and sprinkle with the cheese.

Bake for 40 minutes, or until the pastry is crisp and lightly golden.

Any leftover pastry can be made into grissini (breadsticks): Roll the pastry out to a ½-inch thickness, cut it into long, ½-inch-wide strips, and bake at 400°F for 12 minutes. For the cheese in this recipe, I recommend aged pecorino. In Italy, pecorino comes fresh, semi-aged, or aged. The fresh cheese is quite soft, whereas the aged version is much stronger-flavored and harder-textured, making it easy to grate. You could also use ricotta salata in place of the pecorino here. Ricotta salata is a very hard, salty version of ricotta cheese.

CROSTATA DI CICORIA
CHICORY PIE

Serves six to eight

For the pastry

1½ cups spelt flour

⅓ cup semolina flour

⅓ cup all-purpose flour

1 teaspoon minced chili

Scant 3 tablespoons extra virgin olive oil

1 teaspoon salt

For the filling

2 pounds chicory

2 cloves garlic, unpeeled

¼ cup extra virgin olive oil

½ chili

Leaves from 1 sprig rosemary, chopped

Salt

Place the three types of flour in the food processor with the chili, oil, and salt. Turn on the machine, gradually add about ⅓ cup of water, and process until a soft ball of pastry forms. Wrap it in plastic wrap and refrigerate for 1 hour.

Preheat the oven to 400°F and grease a 9-inch pie plate.

Blanch the chicory in a pot of boiling water, changing the water twice, to remove some of the bitterness. Drain thoroughly and roughly chop it.

Lightly crush the garlic cloves with the flat side of a knife. Place the oil in a skillet with the chili, rosemary, and garlic. Place over medium heat. When the oil is hot, add the chicory and toss it well with the herbs for about 5 minutes. Remove from the heat and cool. Salt to taste.

Divide the pastry into two parts and roll each out to ⅛-inch thick. With one, line the prepared pie plate, leaving some pastry hanging over the side of the plate.

Discard the garlic from the sautéed chicory, and spoon the filling in the pastry. Cover it with the remaining pastry, pressing down to seal. Make holes in the top with a fork and bake for about 30 minutes, until the pastry is golden and crisp.

Serve with a soft, creamy cheese such as crescenza. Tuscans eat various kinds of leaves of the Cichorium *family, which grow like weeds in the countryside—in fact, sometimes they're picked straight from the fields rather than being bought in shops or grown in vegetable gardens. The chicory used in this recipe is the dark green, bitter-leafed* Cichorium intybus. *In some stores it may be called dandelion chicory.*

PRIMO

GNOCCHI DI PATATE
POTATO GNOCCHI

Serves six

2¼ pounds white potatoes

1 egg

1½ teaspoons salt

1½ to 2 cups all-purpose flour

Grated Parmigiano-Reggiano

Sage butter (see Note)

Boil the potatoes with their skins on, then drain them and leave them to cool. Peel and mash them. Add the egg and a little salt and mix it very well with enough flour to make a dough that is compact and can be worked easily with your hands.

Cut the dough into 6 pieces and roll each with your hands into a long sausage shape about 1 inch wide. Cut the rolls into 1-inch lengths. Spread flour over a dish towel and stand the gnocchi on it.

Bring a large pot of salted water to a boil and drop the gnocchi in gently by hand. When they float to the surface, remove them using a slotted spoon and place them on a serving dish.

Serve the gnocchi with grated Parmigiano-Reggiano and sage butter.

Gnocchi are dumplinglike creations that are a welcome alternative to the usual pasta. They're simple to make, and very rewarding, but they're best made the moment before they go into the pot to cook. If you find you've made too many, cook them all, toss any leftovers with olive oil, and keep them in the refrigerator. They can be heated briefly in boiling water the following day and served with the sauce of your choice.

The classic way of serving gnocchi is with butter and sage. For each serving, gently melt about 1 tablespoon of butter with 3 or 4 whole sage leaves; cook over low heat for 3 to 4 minutes, and pour the sage butter over the steaming gnocchi.

PRIMO

ZUPPA DEL CASTELLO
VICARELLO SOUP

Serves six

½ cup extra virgin olive oil

6 scallions (including green parts), finely chopped

6 wild fennel bulbs (or 1 store-bought), finely chopped

6 baby artichokes (preferably the *violetto* variety), stalks removed and chopped

6 medium new potatoes, peeled and left whole

6 small spring onion bulbs, peeled and left whole

¼ cup chopped parsley

1 clove garlic, chopped

Salt

Finely chopped fresh chili or grated Parmigiano-Reggiano for serving

Heat 2 tablespoons of the olive oil in a large saucepan. Place over very low heat, add the scallions, fennel, and artichoke stalks, and cook for 30 minutes.

Remove the tough outer leaves from the artichokes and cut off the hard tips of the remaining leaves. Add the artichokes, potatoes, and onions to the pot, along with the parsley, garlic, the remaining oil, and enough water just to cover the ingredients. Season with salt.

Cover and continue cooking for about 25 minutes, until the vegetables are fork-tender.

Serve sprinkled with chopped fresh chili or grated Parmigiano-Reggiano.

This marvelous recipe was one of the first I ever learned, as a young girl, and it has been featured on my springtime dining table ever since. The particularly strong flavor of violetto artichokes—which have thorny tips but no choke at all—are perfect for this dish.

PRIMO

RISOTTO DI ASPARAGI
ASPARAGUS RISOTTO

Serves four

1¾ pounds asparagus, trimmed

2 tablespoons extra virgin olive oil

1 small onion, minced

1¾ cups Vialone Nano rice

1 cup dry white wine

4 cups Meat Stock (page 164) or Vegetable Stock (page 222), hot

2 tablespoons butter

3 tablespoons grated Parmigiano-Reggiano

Cut the asparagus spears into 1-inch pieces, reserving the tips.

Heat the oil in a large saucepan over low heat. Add the onion and sauté for 2 minutes. Add the asparagus pieces minus the tips and cook, covered, for about 10 minutes, stirring frequently and adding a little hot water if the skillet starts to dry out.

Add the rice and stir it with the asparagus and onion for a minute or two. When it begins to stick to the bottom of the pot, pour in the wine, let it evaporate, and raise the heat to medium. Begin adding the hot stock, one ladleful at a time, allowing the rice to absorb the liquid a little before adding the next. About 10 minutes after you have added the rice, add the asparagus tips.

Cook for about 10 more minutes, until the rice is al dente. Stir in the butter and Parmigiano-Reggiano and leave it to stand for a minute before serving.

Risotto isn't part of the traditional Tuscan repertoire, but I grew up in Lombardy, where it's a staple. My mother made an excellent risotto, and I enjoy using our local Tuscan ingredients in this very northern dish.

PRIMO

TORTELLI MAREMMANI DI RICOTTA E SPINACI
MAREMMAN PASTA FILLED WITH RICOTTA CHEESE AND SPINACH

Serves six to eight

½ pound spinach

1 cup sheep's milk ricotta

Ground cinnamon

Salt and freshly ground black pepper

Tortelli Dough (page 38)

Fresh tomato sauce (page 106)

Grated Parmigiano-Reggiano, for serving

Boil the spinach in a small pot of water until wilted, drain and squeeze it to remove the water, and finely chop it.

Place in a bowl and add the ricotta, a generous sprinkling of cinnamon, and salt and pepper to taste. Mix well. This is the filling for the tortelli.

On one strip of the tortelli dough, place 2 heaping tablespoons of the filling at regular intervals every 3 inches, then lay another strip on top. With your fingers, gently press as much air as possible out from between the strips, then cut them with a knife or pastry wheel between the lumps of filling, and press them well to seal. The tortelli should each measure about 3 by 3 inches. You should have about 20 tortelli.

(You can freeze the tortelli at this point, for later use. Spread them on a baking tray in a single layer on parchment paper. When frozen hard, they should be placed in an airtight container.)

Bring a large pot of salted water to a boil and cook the tortelli for about 8 minutes, until they float to the surface. Drain and serve with fresh tomato sauce and a dusting of grated Parmigiano-Reggiano.

This recipe was given to me by the women in our nearest village, Poggi del Sasso, though I have altered it slightly over the years. Allow two of these large tortelli per person. Instead of the fresh tomato sauce, you may choose instead to serve the tortelli with sage leaves that have been fried in a little butter.

SFOGLIA PER TORTELLI
TORTELLI DOUGH

Yields about one-half pound

1½ cups all-purpose flour

¾ cup semolina flour

3 eggs

1 tablespoon extra virgin olive oil

Salt

Place the two flours in a mixer and add the eggs, oil, and a pinch of salt. Work the dough until it is smooth and starts to come together into a ball. Place it in a bowl and cover with plastic wrap or wrap the dough itself in plastic wrap. Leave it in the refrigerator for 1 to 24 hours.

With a rolling pin or a pasta-making machine, roll out strips 3 inches wide by 3 feet long.

CREMA DI LATTUGA
CREAM OF LETTUCE SOUP

Serves four to six

2 cups milk

2 cups Meat Stock (page 164) or Vegetable Stock (page 222)

Leaves from 3 heads butterhead lettuce

3½ tablespoons butter

2 tablespoons breadcrumbs

1 egg yolk

¼ cup grated Parmigiano-Reggiano

In a saucepan, bring the milk and stock to a boil and add the lettuce leaves. Remove the leaves with a slotted spoon before they get completely soft. Place them in a blender and blend until smooth.

Melt the butter in a skillet over medium heat and brown the breadcrumbs, then add them to the stock, along with the blended lettuce. Cook for 15 minutes.

Beat the egg yolk with the Parmigiano-Reggiano in a soup tureen, then pour the soup over it and mix it in.

Serve this soup with a handful of freshly shelled fava beans; 8 per person should do. Alternatively, serve it with 2 scallops per diner (drizzle them with butter and bake them at 350°F for 15 minutes).

PRIMO

CARBONARA CON CARCIOFI E FAVE
CARBONARA PASTA WITH ARTICHOKES AND FAVA BEANS

Serves four

6 baby artichokes, heads and stalks separated

Lemon juice

1 pound fava beans

3 cloves garlic, unpeeled

¼ cup extra virgin olive oil

3 slices pancettà, diced

Salt

1 egg plus 3 egg yolks

1 chili, minced

¾ pound fusilli pasta

Leaves from 1 bunch parsley, minced

Grated Parmigiano-Reggiano for serving

Discard the outer leaves and the hard tips from the artichoke heads, then cut them into thick slices. Put them in water with lemon juice to keep them from turning brown. Peel the stringy outer layer from the artichoke stalks, cut them into small pieces, and put them in the lemon water with the rest.

Remove the fava beans from their pods, drop them into a pot of boiling water for 30 seconds, then drain and remove their shells.

Crush the garlic cloves with the flat side of a knife and place in a high-sided skillet along with the oil. Place over medium heat and sauté for 2 minutes. Turn up the heat, add the pancetta, and cook for about 5 minutes, stirring frequently.

Drain the artichokes and add them to the skillet with 2 tablespoons water. Lower the heat slightly, cover, and cook for 7 to 8 minutes, stirring gently a couple of times. Season with salt, remove the garlic, and continue cooking, uncovered, for another minute or two, until there is hardly any juice left in the bottom of the pan. Add the parsley.

In a soup tureen, beat the whole egg and the yolks with the chili and a pinch of salt.

Bring a large pot of salted water to a boil and cook the pasta until it is al dente. Keeping some of the cooking water aside, drain the pasta and add it to the skillet with the artichokes and beans. Mix well over low heat.

Transfer the pasta and artichokes to the soup tureen and stir it into the eggs, adding a little of the pasta cooking water, if necessary, to make a smooth sauce.

Serve piping hot with grated Parmigiano-Reggiano.

PRIMO

MALTAGLIATI CON RAGÙ DI FRUTTI DI MARE, FAVE E PISELLI
PASTA WITH SEAFOOD, FAVA BEANS, AND PEAS

Serves six

For the pasta

1½ cups all-purpose flour

1 cup semolina flour

3 eggs

1 tablespoon extra virgin olive oil

Salt

For the sauce

1 pound mixed mussels, clams, and other bivalves

6 tablespoons extra virgin olive oil

1 clove garlic, coarsely chopped

2 cloves garlic, crushed

12 shrimp

1 cup peeled fava beans

⅔ cup peas, cooked

Leaves from 1 bunch marjoram and thyme, finely chopped

Mix the two flours on a work surface, make a heap with a well in the center, and break the eggs into the well. Add the oil and a pinch of salt, then gently work the ingredients together with a fork. When the flour has absorbed the other ingredients, knead the mixture very well until it forms a smooth, soft dough. Cover the dough with a bowl and let it rest for 30 minutes.

Take one third of the dough and roll it out on a floured surface, turning it frequently to prevent it from sticking. When it is thin enough to be translucent when held up to the light, cut it into irregularly shaped pieces and set them aside on a well-floured baking sheet. Repeat this process with the rest of the dough.

Clean the seafood well and cook in a saucepan over high heat with 2 tablespoons of the oil and the chopped garlic until the shells have opened. Remove from the heat, then remove the seafood from the shells and cool. Strain the liquid from the saucepan and reserve. Chop the seafood.

Place one of the garlic cloves in a skillet along with 2 more tablespoons of the oil. Place over medium heat, add the shrimp, and cook for 2 minutes. Place the remaining garlic clove in another skillet with the remaining 2 tablespoons oil, along with the fava beans and peas. Cover the skillet and cook for a few minutes, then remove the cover, add the chopped seafood, and cook for 2 minutes, stirring well.

Bring a large pot of salted water to a boil and cook the pasta until it is al dente. Drain. Add the pasta to the seafood sauce and toss for a few minutes over high heat, pouring in some of the liquid from the shells, if necessary. Add salt to taste, sprinkle with the thyme and marjoram, and arrange the shrimp on top.

SECONDO

CONIGLIO CON LE OLIVE
RABBIT WITH OLIVES

Serves six

2 cloves garlic, unpeeled

1½ tablespoons butter

3 tablespoons extra virgin olive oil

15 sage leaves, minced

1 rabbit, cut into 12 pieces

1 branch rosemary

1 cup dry white wine

1 large onion, grated

Salt and freshly ground black pepper

Meat Stock (page 164), as needed

½ cup pitted black olives, preferably *taggiasche*

3 tablespoons pine nuts

Crush the garlic cloves with the flat side of a knife.

Combine the garlic, butter, oil, and sage in a skillet. Place over low heat and cook for a minute or two to melt the butter.

Add the rabbit pieces and rosemary and continue cooking, stirring frequently, until the rabbit turns a golden color. Add the wine and stir until it evaporates.

Add the onion to the rabbit mixture. Season with salt and pepper and cook, covered, over low heat for about 1½ hours, adding a little stock from time to time if it starts to dry out. Add the olives and pine nuts halfway through cooking. Remove the garlic and rosemary before serving.

Small black taggiasche *olives were originally cultivated by Benedictine monks in the northwestern Liguria region. They are usually sold in brine, ready to be eaten as they are, or used in cooking to add a decisive olive flavor to dishes.*

Serve this dish with Pan-Cooked Artichokes (page 44) and mashed potatoes.

CONTORNO

CARCIOFI IN TEGAME
PAN-COOKED ARTICHOKES

Serves six

12 baby artichokes (preferably the *violetto* variety; see Note, page 32)

¼ cup extra virgin olive oil

2 cloves garlic, chopped

Leaves from 1 bunch parsley, chopped, plus more for serving

Salt and freshly ground black pepper

Wash the artichokes, remove the hard outer leaves, and cut off the pointed ends.

Place the artichokes in a saucepan with the oil, garlic, parsley, and salt and pepper to taste. Place over low heat, add 1 cup water, cover the pan, and cook for 8 to 10 minutes, until the artichokes are tender. Serve sprinkled with parsley.

Artichokes are everywhere in spring: small, fresh, and delicious. In Tuscany we eat them in many different ways. The smallest and best we leave raw, slice very thinly, and eat in salads (see page 22) and pinzimonio (crudités). *Otherwise, we cook them in various ways that always amaze our foreign guests at Vicarello. We never boil them and, as they're so tender, we always eat the whole thing—including the choke, which won't have formed if the artichokes are small enough—rather than just pick at the leaves. To achieve the same effect, you'll have to use the most tender of baby artichokes—or find an Italian market gardener who will grow them for you!*

CONDIMENTO

SALE AROMATICO
AROMATIC SALT

Yields four pounds

Leaves from 1 bunch rosemary

Leaves from 1 bunch sage

Leaves from 1 bunch thyme

½ head garlic, peeled

10 bay leaves

4 pounds (about 9 cups) sea salt

Mince all the herbs, leaving the peeled garlic cloves and a few bay leaves whole. Place in a bowl and add the salt; mix well. Cover the bowl and set aside for 1 week, stirring a couple of times a day. Store the salt in glass jars.

I make this flavored salt twice a year and use it frequently in many meat dishes. The very best salt for this purpose, I find, is sea salt from Sicily—though my preference could be due to the fact that this is Italy's best and I'm Italian! Atlantic sea salt is good too; in fact, any untreated sea salt is just fine. The aromatic salt is better if it's left to sit for a couple of months before using.

SECONDO

AGNELLO AL LATTE
LAMB BAKED IN MILK

Serves four

3½ tablespoons butter, softened

Leaves from 1 bunch sage, finely chopped

1 clove garlic

Large pinch Aromatic Salt (opposite)

1 leg of lamb, about 8 pounds

2 tablespoons extra virgin olive oil

1¼ cups milk

Preheat the oven to 350°F.

Beat 1½ tablespoons of the butter with the sage, garlic, and aromatic salt. With a sharp knife, make deep cuts in the lamb every 3 inches and fill them with the butter and sage mixture.

Melt the remaining 2 tablespoons butter with the oil in a high-sided ovenproof dish, put the leg of lamb into it, and cover it with a lid or aluminum foil. Bake for 30 minutes.

Remove the cover and bake for an additional 20 minutes, then add the milk and return to the oven for about 30 minutes, until the lamb and its sauce are golden.

What we in Tuscany simply call lamb is called spring lamb in the United States. Only the youngest, most tender lamb should be used in this recipe. Serve this dish with Fricaseed Artichokes (page 48) and spring salad with primrose and violet flowers.

CONTORNO

SECONDO

CARCIOFI IN FRICASSEA
FRICASSEED ARTICHOKES

Serves four

8 baby *violetto* artichokes (see Note, page 32)

1 clove garlic, unpeeled

3 tablespoons extra virgin olive oil

1 egg plus 2 egg yolks

Salt and freshly ground black pepper

½ cup grated Parmigiano-Reggiano

¼ cup chopped parsley

Juice of ½ lemon

Wash the artichokes, remove the hard outer leaves, and cut off the thorny ends of the leaves. Cut each into 6 pieces.

Crush the garlic clove with the flat side of a knife, place it in a skillet with the oil and artichokes, and cook over medium heat for 5 minutes.

Beat the whole egg and yolks in a bowl and season with salt and pepper. Mix in the Parmigiano-Reggiano and parsley, and pour the mixture over the artichokes as they continue to cook over medium heat. Cook until the sauce is thickened, about 3 minutes, then drizzle with the lemon juice. Remove the garlic before serving.

TORTINO DI CARCIOFI
ARTICHOKE OMELETTE

Serves four

6 baby *violetto* artichokes (see Note, page 32)

¼ cup all-purpose flour

3 tablespoons extra virgin olive oil

4 eggs

¼ cup milk

Salt

¼ cup chopped parsley

Wash the artichokes, discard the tough outer leaves and most of the stalk, cut the artichokes lengthwise into ¼-inch slices, and dip the slices in the flour. Heat the oil in a skillet over medium heat and cook the artichokes until golden, turning occasionally.

In a bowl, beat the eggs, milk, and a pinch of salt, then add the chopped parsley and pour the mixture over the artichokes. Cook over medium heat for a few minutes, until the omelette sets.

Don't flip the omelette: if you wish to cook the top more, cover and leave it for another minute or two.

After all these years, Carlo and I still disagree about omelettes. In Lombardy, where I'm from, we make omelettes with a lot of eggs and we flip them; Tuscans make them with fewer eggs and cook them only on one side, leaving the top soft and slightly uncooked. This recipe, however, is definitely a Tuscan-style omelette.

SECONDO

SPINACINO O TASCA DI VITELLO RIPIENA
STUFFED VEAL

Serves six

1¾ pound veal breast

1 slice stale bread, broken into pieces

⅓ cup milk

1⅓ cups shelled peas

Salt

2 eggs

¼ pound slice of ham or 2 fresh sausages, diced

Leaves from 1 bunch parsley, minced

3 tablespoons grated Parmigiano-Reggiano

Freshly ground black pepper

2 tablespoons butter

2 tablespoons extra virgin olive oil

Ask your butcher to cut a horizontal "pouch" for the filling in the center of the veal breast.

Preheat the oven to 350°F. Soak the bread in the milk for a few minutes.

Cook the peas in salted boiling water for 15 minutes; drain.

Mash up the bread and drain off the excess milk, then mix the bread with the peas, eggs, ham, parsley, and Parmigiano-Reggiano. Season with salt and pepper to taste. Place this mixture inside the veal "pouch," and sew up the opening.

Melt the butter in the oil in a flameproof baking dish over medium heat. Add the veal and cook, turning frequently, until it begins to color. Transfer to the oven and bake for about 1 hour, until the juices run clear when the veal is pierced through with a fork.

I have two local butchers whom I've come to know well over the years. Visits to their shops always involve long chats about the meat they have to offer and the way I want it prepared. A friendly relationship with an old-fashioned butcher is essential if your meat dishes are going to be really special.

Serve this dish with New Potatoes with Rosemary (page 52) and Pan-Cooked Spring Vegetables (page 52).

CONTORNO

CONTORNO

PATATE NOVELLE AL ROSMARINO
NEW POTATOES WITH ROSEMARY

Serves six

3½ pounds small new potatoes

3 tablespoons extra virgin olive oil

Large pinch Aromatic Salt (page 46)

1 sprig rosemary

Preheat the oven to 400°F.

Without peeling the potatoes, wash them, dry them, and place them on a baking sheet. Toss with the oil, aromatic salt, and rosemary.

Bake for 1 hour without turning, until the potatoes are tender and golden.

CASSERUOLA PRIMAVERILE
PAN-COOKED SPRING VEGETABLES

Serves six

2½ pounds fava beans

12 asparagus spears, trimmed

6 baby artichokes

Juice of 1 lemon

2 tablespoons extra virgin olive oil

2 shallots, thinly sliced

Leaves from 1 sprig mint

Remove the fava beans from their pods, plunge them into a pot of boiling water for 30 seconds, then drain them and remove their shells. Cut the asparagus spears into 1-inch pieces.

Wash the artichokes, discard the tough outer leaves and the thorny tips, and cut them into thin lengthwise slices. Dip the slices into a bowl of water mixed with the lemon juice to keep them from turning brown. Drain them and dry with paper towels. Place them in a skillet with the oil and sauté over medium heat for 5 minutes.

Add the fava beans, asparagus, and 3 tablespoons of water and cook, covered, for 7 minutes. Remove the cover, add the shallots and mint leaves, and cook for 1 minute more.

SECONDO

CONTORNO

BOCCONCINI DI AGNELLO
HERBED LAMB BUNDLES

Serves six

1 leg of lamb, about 2 pounds

1 pork caul

Leaves from 1 bunch each rosemary, sage, and thyme, minced

2 cups (4 sticks) butter

Remove the meat from the bone and cut it into 1-inch cubes. (You might want to ask your butcher to do this for you.) Cut the caul into pieces large enough to wrap around the individual lamb pieces.

Sprinkle the herbs over the cubes of meat and mix them in well. Wrap each piece of meat in a piece of caul and secure it with a toothpick.

Melt the butter in a large saucepan over low heat. With a slotted spoon, skim off and discard the froth that rises to the surface. Raise the heat to medium. Lower the lamb pieces into the pan and deep-fry them in the butter for about 5 minutes, until they turn golden. Drain the lamb well and serve.

Pork caul is the fatty, lacy membrane that encases the animal's internal organs.

Serve this dish with Green Beans with Pancetta (opposite) and Aromatic Herb Salad (page 55).

FAGIOLINI AVVOLTI NELLA PANCETTA
GREEN BEANS WITH PANCETTA

Serves six

2 cups trimmed green beans

2 tablespoons extra virgin olive oil, plus more for the bacon

Leaves from 2 sprigs savory, minced

Salt and freshly ground black pepper

6 slices pancetta, each cut in half

Cook the green beans in a pot of boiling water until they are still just slightly al dente; very fresh beans should take about 4 minutes. Drain.

Heat the oil in a skillet over medium heat, toss the beans in the oil for a couple of minutes, then add the savory and season with salt and pepper to taste.

Divide the beans into 12 portions and wrap each in a half slice of pancetta. Secure the pancetta in place with a toothpick. Toss the "parcels" with a little oil in the pan. Cook over medium heat for a few minutes, turning, until the pancetta is crisp and golden.

For this recipe we use pancetta stesa or rigatino, but you may use bacon.

CONTORNO

INSALATINA CON ERBE AROMATICHE
AROMATIC HERB SALAD

Serves four to six

½ pound baby lettuce

Leaves from 2 small bunches of herbs
(see Note), minced

3 tablespoons extra virgin olive oil

2 teaspoons balsamic vinegar

Salt and freshly ground black pepper

Toss the lettuce with the herbs in a salad bowl.

In a small bowl, whisk together the oil and
vinegar, season with salt and pepper, and toss
with the lettuce and herbs.

*For the herbs, I choose from the following,
depending on what looks best in the garden:
chervil, chives, marjoram, oregano, tarragon,
and thyme.*

CASSERUOLA DI PISELLINI CON PROSCIUTTO E LATTUGA
PEAS WITH HAM AND LETTUCE

Serves six

1 clove garlic, unpeeled

2 pounds peas in their pods, shelled

1 shallot, sliced into thin rings

5-ounce slice Parma ham, diced

¼ cup extra virgin olive oil

Salt and freshly ground black pepper

8 lettuce leaves

Crush the garlic clove with the flat side of
a knife.

In a large saucepan, combine the garlic, peas,
shallots, ham, oil, and ⅔ cup water. Season
with salt and pepper and cover with the lettuce
leaves. Cover the saucepan and cook over
medium heat for 15 to 20 minutes. Remove and
discard the garlic before serving.

SECONDO

POLLO IN FRICASSEA
FRICASEED CHICKEN

Serves six

1 whole chicken, about 2½ pounds

2 tablespoons butter

2 tablespoons extra virgin olive oil

1 small onion, finely chopped

Meat Stock (page 164), as needed

Salt and freshly ground black pepper

3 egg yolks

2 tablespoons finely chopped parsley leaves

Juice of 1 lemon

Cut the chicken into 14 pieces: 2 drumsticks, 2 wings, the breast quartered, the 2 thighs each halved, and the back halved. Wash the chicken pieces.

In a large skillet, melt the butter in the oil over low heat. Add the onion and sauté for 5 minutes. Add the chicken pieces and cook, turning them constantly, until they are golden. Add a little stock, season with salt and pepper, and continue cooking over low heat for about 20 minutes, adding more stock if it starts to dry out.

Beat the egg yolks, add the parsley, and season with pepper. Off the heat, pour this sauce over the steaming chicken pieces and continue turning them. Add the lemon juice and turn again. Serve immediately.

There's no getting around it: a free-range chicken will always taste so much better than an industrially raised bird. Free-range chickens have tough bones and the flesh is far more compact. I raise my own, but sometimes I get too fond of my stock, and I allow them to get too old for cooking. On a rare occasion I'll get one from a neighbor.

Serve this dish accompanied by Peas with Ham and Lettuce (page 55).

SECONDO

ORATA AL FINOCCHIETTO SELVATICO
BREAM WITH WILD FENNEL

Serves four

1 sea bream, about 2½ pounds

Salt and freshly ground black pepper

1 large bunch wild fennel leaves

2½ cups dry white wine

5 juniper berries

4 cherry tomatoes, cut in half

¼ cup extra virgin olive oil

Season the inside cavity of the bream with salt and pepper and stuff it with a handful of the fennel leaves.

Make a stock: In a large, wide pot, combine 2 cups wine, 2 cups water, the juniper berries, and half the remaining fennel leaves. Bring to a simmer, and add the tomatoes and fish. Cover and steam until the fish is just cooked through (the flesh should flake easily and be opaque), about 20 minutes.

In a heatproof bowl or pot, whisk the oil with the remaining ½ cup wine and season with salt and pepper. Finely chop the remaining fennel leaves, add them to the bowl or pot, and place inside a larger saucepan that is half filled with water. Heat the mixture by bringing the water to a gentle boil.

To fillet the fish, use a sharp knife and ease the flesh off the backbone along one side, working from the head toward the tail. At this point, you can either turn the fish over and repeat on the other side, or remove the backbone, starting from the head, then scrape away any remaining smaller bones left behind in the second fillet. Arrange these two pieces on a warmed serving plate and drizzle the oil and fennel sauce over them.

If you can't find wild fennel, substitute this ingredient with the frondy leaves from fennel bulbs.

Serve this dish with steamed new potatoes dressed with olive oil, salt, and a little chopped parsley.

DOLCE

PLUMCAKE
PLUMCAKE

Serves six to eight

¼ cup golden raisins

2 cups all-purpose flour

1 cup plus 2 tablespoons sugar

1½ teaspoons baking powder

2 tablespoons butter, softened

¼ cup milk

½ cup plain yogurt

Grated zest of 1 lemon

¼ cup vegetable oil

2 eggs, separated

10 pitted prunes, quartered

4 dried figs, quartered

Salt

¼ cup coarsely chopped hazelnuts

Preheat the oven to 325°F and line a 9 x 5-inch loaf pan with parchment paper.

Soak the golden raisins in warm water for about 10 minutes.

In a mixer, combine 1¾ cups of the flour, 1 cup of the sugar, the baking powder, butter, milk, yogurt, lemon zest, oil, and egg yolks, and mix until smooth.

Dry the golden raisins, dip them in the remaining ¼ cup flour, and shake off any excess; mix them with the prunes and figs and add them to the mixer bowl; fold into the mixture.

Beat the egg whites with a pinch of salt until stiff peaks form. Fold them gently into the mixture. Transfer it to the prepared loaf pan.

Mix the hazelnuts with the remaining 2 tablespoons sugar to make a topping, and sprinkle over the cake.

Bake for about 55 minutes, until a crunchy golden top has formed and a toothpick inserted into the center comes out clean. Let cool on a rack for 10 minutes before removing the cake from the pan. Let the cake cool completely on a rack.

Despite its name, this is a very Italian recipe. This very light version is particularly good for children's snacks. Plumcake needn't have anything to do with fruit: you can make a "black and white" plumcake by omitting the dried fruits, dividing the batter in two, adding 3 or 4 tablespoons of cocoa powder to one half, then putting both parts separately in the cake pan. Stir them gently if you'd like to obtain a marbled effect.

DOLCE

TORTA MARIA
MARIA'S CHOCOLATE CAKE

Serves six to eight

10 egg whites

Salt

1 cup sugar

7 ounces dark chocolate, in pieces

1¼ cups hazelnuts

Preheat the oven to 350°F. Grease a high-sided 10-inch round cake pan and line it with parchment.

In a mixer, beat the egg whites with a pinch of salt until stiff peaks form.

In a food processor, process the sugar, chocolate, and hazelnuts for a few seconds, until they're coarsely chopped. Fold together with the egg whites and place in the prepared baking pan.

Smooth the top of the mixture and bake for 35 minutes. To check that it's done, insert a skewer into the center of the cake: it should come out mostly clean, though the egg white and chocolate mixture makes this cake very moist, which means it will leave a little more batter on the skewer than drier cakes. Let the cake cool for 10 minutes on a rack before removing from the pan. Serve warm or let cool completely on a rack.

I was given the recipe for this magic cake by Maria, the mother of a school friend of my son Brando. He talked about it constantly, until Maria brought me both the cake and the recipe. You can change the end result by varying the amount of egg white or by chopping the chocolate and nuts more or less finely.

DOLCE

AMOR POLENTA
ALMOND CORNMEAL CAKE

Serves six

½ cup peeled almonds

1 tablespoon superfine sugar

½ cup (1 stick) butter, softened

1¼ cups confectioners' sugar

2 eggs plus 2 yolks

½ cup fine cornmeal

½ cup all-purpose flour

1½ teaspoons baking powder

1 tablespoon maraschino liqueur, or 4 amaretti cookies, crumbled

Preheat the oven to 350°F and grease a 9 x 5-inch loaf pan.

In a food processor, combine the almonds with the superfine sugar and process to a fine powder.

In a mixer, beat the butter with 1 cup of the confectioners' sugar. Continue beating as you add—one by one—the 2 whole eggs, then the 2 egg yolks.

Sift the cornmeal, flour, and baking powder into a bowl and add it to the egg and sugar mixture. Add the nut mixture and the liqueur.

Turn the mixture into the prepared pan and bake for 35 minutes, or until a skewer inserted gently into the center of the cake comes out clean.

Remove the cake from the oven and turn it upside down onto a wire rack, leaving it to cool in the pan. Remove the cake from the pan and sprinkle with the remaining ¼ cup confectioners' sugar.

This cake is served in all the best cafés in Milan. It's light and delicate, and a slice for breakfast is a very good way to start the day. Maraschino liqueur has been made since the sixteenth century from the fruit, leaves, and pits of marasca cherries, grown in Croatia and northeast Italy.

DOLCE

ZUCCOTTO DI PASQUA
EASTER TRIFLE

Serves ten

For the sponge cake

6 eggs, separated

¾ cup sugar

Salt

1¼ cups all-purpose flour

1 teaspoon baking powder

Grated zest of 1 lemon

For the filling

2 cups heavy cream

2 cups fresh ricotta cheese

1¼ cups confectioners' sugar

4 cups quartered strawberries or halved raspberries, or a combination of the two, plus more for serving

¼ cup Maraschino liqueur

Preheat the oven to 350°F and grease and flour a 9-inch square or round baking pan.

For the sponge cake, beat the egg yolks with the sugar in a bowl. In a separate bowl, beat the egg whites with a pinch of salt until stiff peaks form. Sift the flour and baking powder into another bowl, then mix it into the egg yolks and sugar. Gently fold in the egg whites, then add the lemon zest.

Transfer the mixture to the prepared pan and bake for 35 minutes, or until a skewer inserted gently into the center of the cake comes out clean. Leave to cool in the pan, then cut into ½-inch-thick fingers about 6 inches long.

For the filling, whip the cream. With a spoon, push the ricotta through a sieve into a bowl, then add the confectioners' sugar, whipped cream, and the fruit. Mix very gently.

Line a large Easter-egg mold with plastic wrap, leaving some hanging over the edges of the mold, and line with slices of sponge cake. Mix the liqueur with two tablespoons water, then sprinkle the cake with one third of this mixture. Fill the mold halfway with the ricotta filling, and add another layer of cake, and sprinkle with half of the remaining liqueur mixture. Add more of the ricotta filling. Place one more layer of cake on top and sprinkle with the remaining liqueur mixture.

Cover with plastic wrap and refrigerate for 4 hours, then turn the trifle out onto a serving plate; the wrap used to line the mold will help you to release the trifle from the mold and invert it without mishaps. Garnish with strawberries or raspberries.

If you don't have an appropriate mold, use a deep pudding bowl. Maraschino is a sour cherry liqueur made in Italy.

DOLCE

STRUDEL DELLA NONNA
GRANDMA'S STRUDEL

Serves eight to ten

For the pastry

3⅓ cups all-purpose flour

⅓ cup sugar

¾ teaspoon salt

1 tablespoon extra virgin olive oil

For the filling

¾ cup golden raisins

All-purpose flour for dredging

5 baking apples, unpeeled, cored, and thinly sliced

¾ cup pine nuts

Juice of ½ lemon

¼ cup superfine sugar

2 tablespoons butter, melted

Cinnamon (optional)

Confectioners' sugar for dusting

Combine the pastry ingredients in a food processor along with 1 cup lukewarm water and pulse to make a smooth dough. Remove the bowl, cover, and leave to stand for 1 hour.

Preheat the oven to 350°F.

Soak the raisins in warm water for a few minutes, then drain and dry them, dip them in flour, and remove excess flour by shaking them in a strainer.

In a bowl, mix the apples, raisins, pine nuts, lemon juice, and sugar.

Divide the pastry in half and roll each half out into a ⅛-inch rectangle. Spread half the fruit mixture on each piece of pastry, pour half the melted butter over it, and sprinkle with cinnamon, if using, then roll the pastry around the filling, pressing down firmly to close at the sides. Brush the tops with the remaining melted butter.

Bake for 30 minutes, or until the top of the strudels are golden and crunchy. Cool, dust with confectioners' sugar, and serve.

This strudel recipe comes from my husband's family. It's a kind of phyllo pastry—not quite so thin but equally good. The result is a light, delicious strudel that tends to disappear the moment it's ready.

DOLCE

COLOMBA DI PAN BRIOCHE
BRIOCHE DOVE

Serves eight to ten

2¼ teaspoons (1 envelope) active dry yeast

⅓ cup lukewarm milk

4 cups all-purpose flour

1½ teaspoons salt

5 eggs plus 1 egg yolk, beaten

1 cup (2 sticks) butter, softened

½ cup sugar

1 cup candied citrus fruit, diced

Grated zest of 1 lemon

1 teaspoon orange-flower water

Confectioners' sugar for dusting

In a bowl, add the yeast to the milk and stir until it dissolves.

In a mixer with a dough-hook attachment, combine the flour, salt, 5 whole eggs, and milk mixture, and beat for a few minutes at low speed. Gradually increase the speed until the dough becomes smooth and comes together in a ball.

In a bowl, beat the butter and sugar, and gradually add it to the dough in the mixer, beating slowly at first, then increasing the speed to medium. Add the candied fruit, lemon zest, and orange-flower water and work in briefly. Cover the bowl with a dish towel and leave it to rise at room temperature for 2 hours, or until it has doubled in volume.

Punch down the dough, cover, and leave it to rise in the refrigerator for another 4 hours.

Punch down the dough again, then place it in a buttered 10-inch cake pan. Brush the top with the beaten egg yolk and leave it to rise at room temperature until it has doubled in size, up to 2 hours.

Meanwhile, preheat the oven to 400°F. Place the baking pan in the oven. Bake for 15 minutes, reduce the heat to 350°F, and continue baking for an additional 35 minutes, or until a cake tester inserted in the center comes out clean and the top is golden.

Remove from the oven, cool on a wire rack, then dust with confectioners' sugar.

For a different effect, you can sprinkle the top with sugar crystals or almonds before baking it. Unlike most brioche recipes, this version keeps well and stays very soft. At Easter, we use a baking pan shaped like a dove (colomba) for this traditional cake.

L'ESTATE

L'ESTATE
SUMMER

CASTELLO DI VICARELLO is almost one thousand feet above sea level, but on long days of endless sun, the altitude offers little relief from the dusty heat. Castle guests stretch out beneath shady trees or under pergolas with their gently swaying greenery, making the occasional foray to refresh themselves in one of the two swimming pools on the grounds. Workers—and that includes myself and Carlo of course—cannot afford such luxury. Vicarello is never busier.

Certainly, the castle's cavernous kitchen offers some respite from summer temperatures, but only if the huge gas range that occupies the center of room can be kept turned off. Mercifully, few people can face heavy cooked meals in these conditions.

Salads are the order of the day. The freshest of green leaves are tossed in fine olive oil from the previous winter's pressing, along with anything refreshing the vegetable garden yields that day; a few sprigs of mint add a taste of coolness. From my fridge and cellar storeroom, other summer *stuzzichini* (snacks) appear: Sweet and Sour Eggplant and Peppers (page 90), sun-dried tomatoes preserved with herbs from the garden, and Eggplant with Mint and Yogurt (page 88). A small selection of these seasonal specialties is more than enough to sate appetites in the hottest hours of the dog days.

In the evening, the situation changes as a cool sea breeze begins to blow up the valley from the distant coast. No one rushes to eat early: enjoying the sunset—perhaps with a glass of cold white wine in hand—is a slow pleasure, and the main meal of the day can wait till later in the long, conversation-filled evening.

L'ESTATE
SUMMER

IN THE GARDEN

THE SUMMER GARDEN is a hive of activity: just keeping the lawn in check requires many hours of labor every week. In addition to constant weeding and reframing of the beds, new seedlings must be planted as the first crop ceases to produce. The vegetable garden overflows with cucumbers, zucchini, multicolored peppers, eggplant, sweet-smelling herbs, and salad leaves of all imaginable shapes and sizes. There's so much that, try as they might, not even a houseful of guests could possibly consume it all. So I get down to preserving.

We grow several varieties of tomatoes, each serving its own purpose. The red and yellow cherry tomatoes are caramelized and served with fresh cheese, or simply eaten as snacks out of hand. The plum varieties become *passata*, that staple of Italian cooking, so simple to make (page 86). It delivers a sudden rush of summer perfume each time you twist the top off a jar in the colder months. Regular tomatoes go into Caprese salads, made with oozing, milky mozzarella, or Panzanella—the traditional Tuscan bread salad (page 102).

Sliced and grilled peppers and eggplants can be preserved in olive oil with herbs. The zucchini bloom and bear new squash at an alarming rate, inspiring us to develop new recipes each year. Herbs are picked and hung to dry—or minced and frozen—ready for use in the winter.

The only threat to this abundance is the boars and the porcupines, nocturnal raiders attracted by an easily accessible snack. One recent night we were visited by an entire family of wild boars. The next morning we awoke to find the garden stripped of all its leeks, onions, and parsley! Short of ringing the *orto* with high wire fences, there's no solution except vigilance—and accepting that the fauna of the area deserves its share of this bounty too.

IN THE VINEYARD

CARLO'S VINEYARDS ARE also thriving: it's as if you can see the grapes swelling before your eyes. Here the plants are not trained along horizontal wires but bent over and twisted together to form long rows of pretty vine arches. To protect the precious fruit from the harsh summer sun, Carlo and his helpers pull leaves over the bunches on the hotter southern side, but remove leaves elsewhere to ensure that sufficient light and air circulate to help the grapes develop well.

Wild animals are a problem here too, but where his grapes are concerned, Carlo isn't so tolerant. One hailstorm or an attack of the magpies and we could be in trouble. So, nets are spread over the vines to keep the birds from pecking at the fruit, and the whole staff is placed on badger watch.

ANTIPASTO

CROSTATINE DI PEPERONI E POMODORI SECCHI
BELL PEPPER AND SUN-DRIED TOMATO TARTLETS

Serves six

For the pastry

1¼ cups all-purpose flour

1¼ cups semolina flour

2 tablespoons extra virgin olive oil

½ chili, thinly sliced

10 chives, minced

Leaves from 3 sprigs oregano, minced, or 1 teaspoon dried

Salt and freshly ground black pepper

For the filling

2 cloves garlic, unpeeled

3 tablespoons extra virgin olive oil

½ fresh chili

3 bell peppers (green, red, and yellow), chopped

2 tablespoons salted capers, well rinsed

Salt

6 sun-dried tomatoes in olive oil

6 Anchovies in Olive Oil (page 96)

To make the pastry, place the two types of flour, the oil, chili, chives, oregano, and a generous pinch of salt and pepper in the food processor with a scant ½ cup water. Pulse until the ingredients form a soft, smooth dough. Wrap the dough in plastic wrap and refrigerate for 1 hour.

Preheat the oven to 350°F.

Crush the garlic cloves with the flat side of a knife. In a skillet, heat the oil and add the garlic and chili. Add the peppers and toss briefly; the peppers should remain crunchy. Add the capers and salt to taste. Remove the garlic.

Roll the pastry out into a thin sheet and line six 4-inch pie dishes. In each place some of the chopped sun-dried tomatoes and the pepper mixture; top each with an anchovy.

Bake for about 35 minutes, until the pastry is browned. Serve hot.

These little pies are also good served cold. I always buy sun-dried tomatoes without oil and prepare them myself. I soak them in boiling water for a minute or so, leave them to dry completely (this can take several hours), then steep them in extra virgin olive oil with a little chili and garlic. They'll keep for months in an airtight container.

ANTIPASTO

FIORI DI ZUCCA FRITTI
FRIED ZUCCHINI FLOWERS

Serves six

18 zucchini flowers, 3 per person

¾ cup all-purpose flour

Salt

1 tablespoon extra virgin olive oil

½ cup ice-cold sparkling mineral water

2 cups peanut oil

Wash the zucchini flowers and remove the pistils from inside, if you like. (Some people leave them; it's a matter of taste.) Leave an inch or two of stalk attached, and stand the flowers on a clean dish towel to dry.

In a large bowl, combine the flour, salt, olive oil, and mineral water to make a batter that is neither too runny nor too sticky.

Heat the peanut oil in a saucepan over medium-high heat until it's hot but not smoking. Gently dip the flowers into the batter, allow any excess to drip back into the bowl, then fry the flowers for 2 minutes on each side, or until they are golden and crisp. Remove with a slotted spoon and serve immediately.

My zucchini plants produce countless flowers every summer. Female flowers produce zucchini: you can see the tiny vegetable forming on the stalk beneath the flower. Unproductive male flowers have slimmer, paler stalks—pick these for frying. Sage leaves can also be fried in this way: seal two large sage leaves together with a little anchovy paste, then dip them in batter and fry. We call this uccellini scappati—*birds that have flown away.*

CROSTATA DI LATTUGA
LETTUCE TART

Serves six

For the pastry

8 chives, minced

Leaves from 1 bunch parsley, minced

Leaves from 3 sprigs savory, minced

1 teaspoon dried oregano

1½ cups all-purpose flour

Salt

2 tablespoons extra virgin olive oil

For the filling

8 Anchovies in Olive Oil (page 94)

Leaves from 1 bunch parsley, minced

1 clove garlic, minced

½ chili, thinly sliced

3 tablespoons extra virgin olive oil

Leaves from 2 heads looseleaf lettuce

Leaves from 3 sprigs oregano

Leaves from 3 sprigs savory

Salt

20 small green olives, pitted

In a bowl, combine the chives, parsley, savory, and oregano, and set aside.

Preheat the oven to 375°F.

To make the pastry, combine the flour, pinch of salt, oil, and herbs in a food processor and process, gradually adding just enough room-temperature water—about ⅓ cup—to form a soft ball of green dough.

To make the filling, scrape the salt from the anchovies with a spatula or knife blade and place them in a bowl with the parsley, garlic, and chili.

Heat the oil in a skillet over medium heat. Add the lettuce, oregano, and savory leaves and sauté for 5 minutes, stirring constantly. Season with salt.

Roll the pastry to a ⅛-inch thickness, place it in a 10-inch round baking dish, and fill it with the lettuce mixture. On top, arrange the anchovies and olives. Bake for 35 minutes, or until the pastry is golden. Serve hot, or cool to room temperature, refrigerate, and serve cold.

Lettuce is used—obviously—in salads. But I also like to cook it, using it in soup (see page 38) and as a fresh-tasting filling for this savory tart. If you find the taste of these anchovies too strong, you can use store-bought anchovies in olive oil instead.

82

ANTIPASTO

CROSTONI DI PEPERONI E ACCIUGHE
BELL PEPPER AND ANCHOVY TOAST

Serves six

1 clove garlic

3 tablespoons extra virgin olive oil

1 green pepper, chopped

1 red pepper, chopped

1 yellow pepper, chopped

1 chili (fresh or dried)

2 tablespoons salted capers, well rinsed

Leaves from 1 sprig thyme

Salt

6 large slices country-style bread, toasted

6 anchovies

Crush the garlic clove with the flat side of a knife, peel it, and place it in a skillet along with the oil. Place over high heat, add the bell peppers and chili (if you're using a fresh chili, cut it into large pieces that can be easily removed before serving), and sauté for about 8 minutes, turning frequently. Add the capers, thyme leaves, and salt to taste.

Serve the peppers on slices of toasted country-style bread, with an anchovy on top.

ANTIPASTO/CONTORNO

ZUCCHINE IN SCAPECE
SWEET AND SOUR FRIED ZUCCHINI

Serves six to eight

2 tablespoons of golden raisins

6 medium zucchini

1 or 2 cloves garlic

1 tablespoon extra virgin olive oil

1 red onion, thinly sliced

1 tablespoon sugar

1 tablespoon white wine vinegar

Leaves from 2 sprigs mint

Soak the golden raisins in a bowl of warm water for 10 minutes. Drain.

Using a mandoline or a sharp knife, cut the zucchini lengthwise into thin strips. Crush the garlic clove with the flat side of a knife and place it in a skillet along with the oil. Place over high heat. Add the zucchini and sauté, stirring constantly, for 5 minutes. Transfer the zucchini strips to paper towels to drain.

Add the onion to the skillet with the oil. Reduce heat to medium and sauté until slightly transparent. Add the sugar and vinegar and cook for 1 minute more.

Arrange the zucchini in a deep serving dish and add the mint leaves, onions, and golden raisins. Refrigerate until ready to serve.

Serve this dish cold, directly from the fridge; it is excellent with smoked fish.

CONDIMENTO

ANTIPASTO/PRIMO

PASSATA DI POMODORO
TOMATO PUREE

Yields about six cups

2 cloves garlic

6 pounds ripe plum tomatoes, chopped

3 tablespoons extra virgin olive oil

10 basil leaves

Salt

Crush the garlic cloves with the flat side of a knife.

Put the tomatoes in a saucepan with the oil, garlic, 5 basil leaves, and salt to taste. Cook over low heat until the tomatoes dissolve, about 3 hours. Add the remaining 5 basil leaves just before the sauce is ready.

Put the sauce through a sieve or vegetable mill to remove the tomato skins.

The *passata* will keep in the refrigerator for up to 5 days.

MILLEFOGLIE DI MELANZANE
EGGPLANT MILLE-FEUILLE

Serves six

1 clove garlic

8 ripe San Marzano (plum) tomatoes, diced

3 tablespoons extra virgin olive oil

Leaves from 2 bunches basil

Salt

3 large, round, firm eggplants, cut into ¼-inch-thick crosswise slices

3 ounces aged pecorino, grated

Basil sprigs for garnish

Crush the garlic clove with the flat side of a knife and peel it.

Place the tomatoes in a bowl and toss them with the garlic, the oil, half the basil, and salt to taste.

Heat a heavy cast-iron or stone griddle and grill the eggplant slices (without oil) on both sides. On individual serving plates (or one large platter), place a slice of eggplant, and top with some of the tomato mixture, pecorino, and a few basil leaves. Repeat the layers until all ingredients are used.

Garnish with basil sprigs and serve at room temperature.

MELANZANE ALLA MENTA E YOGURT

EGGPLANT WITH MINT AND YOGURT

Serves six

2 medium eggplants

1 clove garlic

1 sprig mint

Salt

¾ cup yogurt

Toasted country-style bread for serving

Preheat the oven to 375°F.

Place the whole eggplants in the oven and bake for about 40 minutes, until the eggplants are soft and the skin is wrinkled. Remove from the oven. As soon as they are cool enough to touch, remove the skin and seeds. Mince the eggplant flesh with the garlic, mint, and a little salt.

Transfer the eggplant mixture to a bowl and pour the yogurt over the top. Spoon over slices of toasted country-style bread.

This simple sauce is a staple of eastern Mediterranean cuisine. It's a marvelous snack, especially on hot summer days.

PARMIGIANA DI MELANZANE

EGGPLANT BAKED WITH CHEESE

Serves six

2 tablespoons rock salt

3 long, large, firm eggplants, sliced 1 inch thick

1 quart peanut oil

4 cups *passata* (page 86)

5 tablespoons grated Parmigiano-Reggiano

1 pound mozzarella, diced, about 4½ cups

Leaves from 1 bunch basil

Dissolve the rock salt in a large bowl of water. Soak the eggplant slices in the salt water for 30 minutes to remove any bitterness; place a dinner plate on top of the slices to keep them submerged. Drain the eggplant slices and dry them with paper towels.

Preheat the oven to 375°F.

Heat the oil in a large skillet over medium-high heat. Add the eggplant slices and fry them until they just start to turn golden. Remove from the oil and set them on paper towels to drain.

In a large ovenproof dish, arrange half of the eggplant, followed by a layer of half of the *passata*, Parmigiano-Reggiano, mozzarella, and basil leaves. Repeat the layers once more with the remaining ingredients. Transfer to the oven and bake for 20 minutes.

This recipe is used all over central and southern Italy, varying a bit from region to region. This version is particularly light, and it can also be made without the mozzarella.

ANTIPASTO/CONTORNO

CAPONATA CON PEPERONI
SWEET AND SOUR EGGPLANT AND PEPPERS

Serves six to twelve

⅓ cup golden raisins

Salt

3 large eggplants, cut into small cubes

2 cups plus 5 tablespoons extra virgin olive oil

1 green pepper, diced

1 red pepper, diced

1 yellow pepper, diced

1 large red onion, thinly sliced

1 stalk celery, chopped

¼ cup salted capers, well rinsed

½ pound small pitted green olives

⅓ cup pine nuts

1½ cups *passata* (page 86)

Leaves from 1 bunch basil

Freshly ground black pepper

2 tablespoons sugar

½ cup red wine vinegar

Soak the golden raisins in a bowl of warm water for 10 minutes. Drain.

Dissolve 1 tablespoon of salt in a large bowl of water. Place the eggplant cubes in the water and soak for 1 hour to remove any bitterness.

Drain the eggplant cubes and dry them well with paper towels. Heat 2 cups of the oil in a skillet over medium-high heat, add the eggplant, and sauté for 5 minutes, or until just turning golden. Remove from the skillet with a slotted spoon and transfer to paper towels to drain.

In the same oil, sauté the peppers over medium-high heat for 5 minutes, turning constantly. Transfer to paper towels to drain.

In a large, clean skillet, heat the remaining 5 tablespoons oil over medium heat. Add the onion and sauté until transparent. Add the celery, capers, olives, pine nuts, and the drained golden raisins; cook for 3 to 4 minutes, stirring constantly. Add the *passata* and basil leaves and season with salt and pepper. Cook, stirring, for 5 minutes.

In a small bowl, dissolve the sugar in the vinegar, then add it to the skillet, stirring thoroughly. Add the peppers and eggplant to the skillet, reduce the heat to low, and cook, stirring, for 3 minutes. Remove from the heat and cool completely before serving.

This wonderful summer dish can be served as an antipasto or a whole meal at lunchtime. It goes well with sharp, seasoned cheeses or with cured fish or meat. It will keep in the refrigerator for a week or more in an airtight container. I "stole" this recipe from Sicily, where it is a traditional dish. It may not be Tuscan, but it's a marvelous summer dish anywhere.

ZUCCHINE RIPIENE
STUFFED ZUCCHINI

Serves four to six

6 zucchini

1 clove garlic, unpeeled

3 tablespoons extra virgin olive oil

1 (5-ounce) can tuna, in olive oil

3 anchovies in oil, diced

2 tablespoons salted capers, well rinsed

Leaves from 1 bunch each basil and parsley, minced

Salt and freshly ground black pepper

3 tablespoons breadcrumbs

2 cups peanut oil

2 cups *passata* (page 86), plus more for serving

Basil sprigs for garnish

Preheat the oven to 375°F.

Cut 4 of the zucchini in half lengthwise and scoop out the seeds and most of the pulp with a spoon. Dice the pulp and the remaining 2 whole zucchini.

Crush the garlic clove with the flat side of a knife and place it in a skillet along with the olive oil. Place over medium heat and sauté for 2 minutes, stirring constantly. Remove the garlic from the skillet and add the zucchini; sauté for 7 to 8 minutes. Transfer the zucchini to a bowl and drain off any liquid released while cooking.

Add the tuna, anchovies, capers, basil, parsley, and salt and pepper to taste; mix well. Fill the scooped-out zucchini halves with the mixture, and sprinkle breadcrumbs on top.

Heat the peanut oil in a skillet over medium-high heat; lower the stuffed zucchini carefully, making sure the oil doesn't flow into the filling. Fry for 5 minutes, or until the vegetables are soft, then stand the zucchini on paper towels to drain.

Heat the *passata* in an ovenproof dish, adding a little water to thin it out. Put the stuffed zucchini into the dish and bake for about 40 minutes.

Serve drizzled with hot passata and topped with fresh basil sprigs.

The small, spherical Tondo di Piacenza *zucchini are the best for this dish, though other types of zucchini will do. This dish is also delicious served cold.*

INSALATA D'ESTATE
SUMMER SALAD

Serves four to six

½ honeydew melon, peeled and seeded

½ cantaloupe, peeled and seeded

4 ripe medium tomatoes

2 oranges

½ head lettuce

1 stalk celery, thinly sliced

1 carrot, grated

3 tablespoons extra virgin olive oil

10 leaves fresh basil

10 leaves fresh mint

Salt and freshly ground black pepper

¼ cup almonds, toasted

3 tablespoons pistachios

Dice the melons and tomatoes. Peel the oranges, slice them into thin rounds, and cut each round in half.

Break up a few of the lettuce leaves to use as garnish; line a salad bowl with the rest.

In a large bowl, toss the fruits and vegetables with the oil. Add the basil and mint leaves and toss again. Season with salt and pepper. Transfer the salad to the lined salad bowl and sprinkle with the almonds and pistachios.

ANTIPASTO

ACCIUGHE SOTTO PESTO
ANCHOVIES IN OLIVE OIL

Yields one-half pound

½ pound salted anchovies

1 clove garlic

Leaves from 1 bunch parsley

Dried chili

Extra virgin olive oil

With a knife, scrape the anchovies several times to remove the salt; don't rinse them.

Mince the garlic, parsley, and dried chili together.

Put a layer of anchovies in the bottom of a jar or crock and spread some of the parsley mixture over it. Repeat until the container is full. Pour enough oil into the jar to cover the anchovies completely.

These anchovies make a great snack on a slice of bread. Store in the refrigerator in an airtight container; they will keep several days.

PANE/ANTIPASTO

ANTIPASTO

FOCACCIA CON CRESCENZA E FIORI DI ZUCCA
FOCACCIA WITH *CRESCENZA* CHEESE AND ZUCCHINI FLOWERS

Serves six

2 cups all-purpose flour

2 cups semolina flour

¼ cup extra virgin olive oil

1 teaspoon salt

14 ounces *crescenza* cheese or any soft, fresh cow's or goat's milk cheese

20 zucchini flowers

4 anchovies

Preheat the oven to 450°F.

Put the two kinds of flour in a mixer with 1 cup water, the oil, and salt. Work for 40 seconds, until a smooth dough forms.

Divide the dough in half and roll each piece out into a rectangle about ⅛ inch thick.

Place one dough half on an oiled baking sheet and spread the *crescenza* cheese over it. Top with the zucchini flowers and anchovies. Cover with the second piece of dough and pinch the edges together so no cheese escapes as it bakes.

Prick the surface of the focaccia here and there with a knife, and bake for 15 minutes. Serve piping hot.

Originally from northern Italy, crescenza *is a creamy, slightly tangy cheese made from cow's milk that is very popular for spreading on bread or focaccia.*

ACCIUGHE FRITTE
FRIED ANCHOVIES

Serves six

1½ pounds fresh anchovies

1 cup milk

¾ cup all-purpose flour

¾ cup extra virgin olive oil

Salt

Lemon wedges for serving

Parsley sprigs for serving

Gut and debone the anchovies, wash and dry them, and place them in a bowl. Cover them with the milk and leave to soak for 30 minutes. Place the flour in a bowl.

Heat the oil in a skillet over medium-high heat. Drain the anchovies, dip them in the flour, and fry them for a minute or two, until they turn golden brown.

Remove the anchovies from the oil using a slotted spoon, allowing as much oil as possible to drip off. Sprinkle the anchovies with salt and serve with lemon wedges and parsley sprigs.

PRIMO

FAZZOLETTI CON RIPIENO DI MELANZANE
PASTA STUFFED WITH EGGPLANT

Serves six

2 long, firm eggplants

Salt

2 cloves garlic

4 tablespoons extra virgin olive oil

1 chili, cut in half

Leaves from 2 sprigs thyme

½ pound cherry tomatoes, cut in half

18 fresh 4 by 4-inch sheets pasta

Simmer the eggplants, whole, in a pot of salted water for 40 minutes, or until they're soft and wrinkled. Drain them, let cool, then cut them lengthwise and discard the seeds and skin. Beat the flesh into a pulp.

Crush the garlic cloves with the flat side of a knife.

Heat 2 tablespoons of the oil in a saucepan over medium heat and add 1 clove of garlic and 1 chili half. When the oil begins to sizzle, add the eggplant flesh and cook for 2 to 3 minutes. Remove the garlic and chili, add half of the thyme leaves, and salt to taste.

Place the tomatoes in a skillet with the remaining clove of garlic, the remaining chili half, and the remaining 2 tablespoons oil. Place over medium heat, cover, and after 5 minutes, when the tomatoes have softened slightly, remove from the heat, remove the garlic, and add the remaining thyme leaves and salt to taste.

Cook the pasta—3 sheets for each diner—in boiling salted water until al dente. Remove the pasta sheets from the water and drain them, taking care not to break them. Place on a serving dish and top each sheet with some of the hot eggplant mixture. Fold each sheet over on itself, like a little handkerchief (*fazzoletti*).

Serve with the tomato sauce.

This is best made with homemade fresh pasta (such as the Tortelli Dough, page 38), but you may instead use dried lasagne sheets cut to size.

PRIMO

MINESTRONE ESTIVO
SUMMER MINESTRONE

Serves six

Salt

3 zucchini, finely chopped

1½ cups finely chopped green beans

1 carrot, finely chopped

1 rib celery, finely chopped

1 onion, finely chopped

1 pound potatoes

1 medium eggplant

1 tomato

¾ cup fresh borlotti (or cranberry) beans

¼ cup extra virgin olive oil, plus more for serving

¾ cup short-grain rice

6 tablespoons Basil Pesto (page 100)

1¼ cup grated Parmigiano-Reggiano

Freshly ground black pepper

In a large saucepan, bring 2 quarts of salted water to a boil. Plunge all the vegetables and the borlotti beans into the saucepan, return to a boil, then reduce the heat, cover, and simmer for 1 hour.

Remove the potatoes, eggplant, and tomato. Without peeling the vegetables, mash the potatoes, eggplant, and tomato well, then return them to the pot. Add the oil and rice. Continue cooking, covered, until the rice is al dente (how long this takes will depend on the type of rice you're using), then turn the heat off and leave the soup to cool with the lid on.

When the soup has cooled, add the pesto, then serve in soup bowls drizzled with olive oil and sprinkled with the Parmigiano-Reggiano and a couple of grinds of black pepper.

This soup is also excellent without the rice; if you omit it, cook down the liquid a bit by simmering with the lid off near the end of cooking. The best rice for this recipe is the round-grain Originale *variety.*

CONDIMENTO

CONDIMENTO

PESTO DI BASILICO
BASIL PESTO

Yields one cup

2 cloves garlic

Coarse salt

60 leaves of basil

1 tablespoon pine nuts

6 tablespoons grated Parmigiano-Reggiano

2 tablespoons grated aged pecorino

½ cup extra virgin olive oil

Put the garlic in a mortar with a few grains of salt, then add the basil leaves, a few at a time, and begin grinding with a circular motion until a green liquid comes out of the leaves. When they are mashed, add the pine nuts, both kinds of cheese, and the oil.

Make pesto as quickly as possible, at a comfortable room temperature. Traditionally it is made in a mortar and pestle; of course, a blender or food processor will do the job faster and much more easily. If you opt for a blender, set the speed as low as possible to avoid heating the pesto too much. Pesto can be kept in a glass jar in the refrigerator; pour a layer of oil over the top to keep it from oxidizing.

Of course pesto is ideal for tossing with pasta; it is also delicious as a seasoning for soups like Minestrone (page 99).

PESTO DI CAPPERI
CAPER SAUCE

Yields one cup

6 tablespoons salted capers

3 tablespoons green olives in brine

3 tablespoons extra virgin olive oil

3 tablespoons pine nuts (optional)

To remove the salt from the capers and olives, soak them in ice-cold water for 50 minutes, changing the water every 10 minutes.

Drain and squeeze the water out of the capers, remove the pits from the olives, and place the capers and olives in a blender. Add the oil and a little water and blend to a creamy paste.

If you're using this sauce to dress pasta, add the pine nuts.

I learned how to make this wonderful summer dish in the Aeolian islands, north of Sicily, where capers grow in great abundance.

PRIMO

PASTA AL SUGO DI COZZE, VONGOLE E FIORI DI ZUCCA
PASTA WITH MUSSELS, COCKLES, AND ZUCCHINI FLOWERS

Serves four to six

2 pounds mussels

2 pounds large cockles (or clams)

20 zucchini flowers

20 cherry tomatoes

6 tablespoons extra virgin olive oil

Leaves from 1 bunch parsley, minced

1 clove garlic, minced

1 chili, minced

1 cup dry white wine

1 pound spaghetti

Wash the mussels and cockles and place them in separate bowls.

Clean the zucchini flowers and stand them on paper towels to dry. Cut a cross into each of the tomatoes, but don't cut them all the way through.

Divide the oil between 2 skillets and place each over medium heat. Add half the parsley, garlic, and chili to each skillet, leaving a little for garnish. When the oil begins to sizzle, pour half the wine into each pan and let it evaporate. Then add the mussels to one pan and the cockles to the other and place 3 tomatoes in each. Cover the pans and cook, shaking the pans from time to time, until the cockles and mussel shells have opened, 7 to 8 minutes.

Remove the shellfish with a slotted spoon, set the cooking liquid aside, and remove most of the mussels and cockles from their shells; leave a few unshelled for garnishing the finished dish.

Strain the cooking liquid from the cockles and mussels into a single bowl.

Boil the pasta in salted water until it is not quite al dente; drain. Place 4 ladles of the shellfish liquid in a large skillet, add the pasta and the remaining tomatoes, and continue cooking until the pasta is al dente. You may need to add more liquid. Shortly before the pasta is ready, add the zucchini flowers and mussels and cockles.

Serve garnished with the reserved cockles, mussels, and remaining parsley, garlic, and chili.

PRIMO

PANZANELLA
TUSCAN BREAD SALAD

Serves six to eight

1 red onion, thinly sliced

3 cucumbers

5 ripe tomatoes, chopped

½ pound lettuce or small chicory salad leaves, chopped

Leaves from 1 bunch basil

5 tablespoons extra virgin olive oil, plus more if needed

1 tablespoon red wine vinegar (optional)

2 pounds slightly stale country loaf (ideally at least 3 days old)

Salt and freshly ground black pepper

Soak the onion in a bowl of water for 1 hour.

Top and tail the cucumbers and rub these pieces vigorously against the cut ends until a white froth appears; this removes any bitter taste. Peel the cucumbers and thinly slice them.

Combine all the vegetables in a bowl and add the basil leaves, the oil, and vinegar, if using.

Break up the bread and dunk it very briefly in a bowl of cold water, until it is soft but not falling apart. Remove the insides, squeeze as much water as possible out of the crust, and place the crust in the bowl with the other ingredients. Season with salt and pepper and add more oil if necessary.

Cover the bowl with plastic wrap and place it in the refrigerator; serve cold.

Panzanella is classic Tuscan peasant food. Some people try to "improve" it by adding eggs or tuna, but I prefer this original Maremman version, which gets even better if left until the following day. It was given to me by the fantastic Olema, mother of nine children.

PRIMO

ZUPPA FREDDA AL POMODORO
CHILLED TOMATO AND BELL PEPPER SOUP

Serves six

¼ red onion, diced

¼ red pepper, diced

¼ yellow pepper, diced

¼ cucumber, peeled and diced

2½ pounds ripe tomatoes, seeded and chopped

2 cloves garlic

1 teaspoon sugar

1 tablespoon red wine vinegar

5 tablespoons extra virgin olive oil

Salt and freshly ground black pepper

2 slices bread, cut into small cubes

Place the onion, bell peppers, and cucumber in a bowl, cover, and refrigerate for at least an hour, or until you are ready to prepare and serve the soup.

Put the tomatoes in a food processor. Add 1 garlic clove, the sugar, vinegar, 3 tablespoons of the oil, and salt and pepper to taste and pulse to combine. Transfer to a bowl, cover, and refrigerate the soup until you're ready to serve it.

Crush the remaining garlic clove with the flat side of a knife, peel it, and place it in a skillet along with the remaining 2 tablespoons oil. Add the bread cubes and sauté until golden, about 3 minutes.

To serve, stir the diced onion, bell pepper, and cucumber into the soup and garnish with the croutons.

You can serve this soup with horseradish for a pungent flavor accent.

PRIMO

SPAGHETTI CON SALSA DI POMODORO AL SOLE
PASTA WITH SUN-BAKED TOMATO SAUCE

Serves six

3 pounds San Marzano (plum) tomatoes

2 cloves garlic, peeled and cut in half

Handful fresh basil leaves

1 fresh chili

¼ cup extra virgin olive oil

Salt

1 pound spaghetti

Using a slotted spoon, dip the tomatoes in a pot of boiling water for 1 minute to loosen the skins. Remove them from the water, cool, then peel them and cut them in half lengthwise. Remove the seeds.

Put the tomato halves in a large bowl and add the garlic, basil leaves, chili, oil, and salt to taste. Mix the ingredients well with your hands, breaking apart the tomatoes, spread the mixture in a salad dish, and put it in the sun for about 90 minutes. Cover with a net to keep insects off.

Cook the pasta in a pot of boiling salted water until it's al dente; drain and serve with the tomato sauce.

These tomatoes are also great on toast. In summer, I often make pasta dishes with uncooked sauces, such as Pasta al Fuoco (page 110) and pasta with Basil Pesto (page 100).

PRIMO

CREMA FREDDA DI ZUCCHINE
CHILLED CREAM OF ZUCCHINI SOUP

Serves four to six

1 clove garlic, unpeeled

3 tablespoons extra virgin olive oil

5 zucchini, diced

Small piece chili, minced

Leaves from 1 sprig mint, minced

Salt and freshly ground black pepper

½ yellow pepper, diced

6 to 8 frozen cubes of Vegetable Stock (page 222)

Croutons for serving

1 firm, ripe tomato, diced

Basil sprigs, for serving

Crush the garlic clove with the flat side of a knife.

Heat 2 tablespoons of the oil with the garlic in a skillet over medium heat. Add the zucchini, increase the heat to high, and cook for about 5 minutes, stirring constantly. Add the chili and mint; season with salt and pepper. Discard the garlic and remove from the heat.

In a separate skillet sauté the pepper in the remaining 1 tablespoon of oil for a couple of minutes; season with salt and set aside.

Keep a few pieces of zucchini whole and blend the rest with enough frozen cubes of stock to make a fairly runny cream. Serve icy cold in individual bowls, garnished with a few croutons, the remaining zucchini pieces, the pepper, tomato, and basil sprigs.

PASTA AL FUOCO
FIERY PASTA

Serves four to six

2 pounds cherry tomatoes, cut in half

3 cloves garlic, peeled and cut in half

2 tablespoons salted capers, well rinsed

2 tablespoons green olives in brine, pitted

1 chili, chopped

Leaves from 3 sprigs basil

5 tablespoons extra virgin olive oil

Freshly ground black pepper

1 pound spaghetti

Salt

1 cup grated baked ricotta or aged pecorino

In a large bowl, combine the tomatoes, garlic, capers, olives, chili, basil leaves, and oil, and season with pepper. Let stand for 1 hour.

Cook the pasta in a large pot of boiling salted water until al dente; drain.

Transfer the pasta to a large bowl, pour the tomato mixture over the pasta, and mix well. Serve with the grated cheese.

Baked ricotta (ricotta infornata) is a Sicilian cheese. Salt is added to fresh ricotta, which is left for about one week then baked until a thin russet brown crust forms. It's delicious grated into vegetable-based pasta sauces and adds a bite to savory pies. If you can't find baked ricotta, you can always replace it with good pecorino.

FAZZOLETTI AL SUGO DI PESCE
PASTA WITH FISH SAUCE

Serves six

5 ripe plum tomatoes

1 clove garlic, unpeeled

Leaves from 2 sprigs parsley, chopped

3 tablespoons extra virgin olive oil

Salt

1 whole fish, such as red snapper, about 1 pound

30 fresh pasta sheets (4 by 4-inch) or ½ pound fresh tagliatelle

Remove the skin and seeds from the tomatoes and cut them into strips (see page 106).

In an oval saucepan, combine the tomatoes, garlic, parsley, and oil; season with salt. Place the fish in the pan and add just enough water to cover the bottom of the pan to a depth of ½ inch. Cover the pan, place over low heat, and cook for 1 hour.

When the fish is cooked, remove the bones and return the flesh to the sauce in the pot.

Cook the pasta in a pot of boiling salted water until it is al dente. Drain.

If you're using pasta sheets, divide the pasta among 6 dinner plates and spoon the sauce over and around the pasta.

If you're using tagliatelle, drain the almost-cooked pasta, keeping a little of the water you cooked the pasta in. Put the tagliatelle into the pan with the fish sauce and finish cooking it there, adding a little of the cooking water if it starts to dry out.

SECONDO

PESCE AL FORNO CON PATATE
BAKED FISH WITH POTATOES

Serves six

2 large white potatoes, peeled and very thinly sliced

1 sea bream or snapper, 2½ pounds

1 clove garlic, unpeeled

2 sprigs parsley

About 3 tablespoons extra virgin olive oil

15 cherry tomatoes

Preheat the oven to 375°F.

Soak the potato slices in a bowl of cold water while you're preparing the rest of the ingredients.

Line an oven pan or a large baking dish with a piece of aluminum foil long enough to fold over and cover the fish completely. Drain the potato slices and put them in the pan, then lay the fish on top. Inside the fish put the garlic, parsley, and a little olive oil. Sprinkle the cherry tomatoes over the fish and potatoes, drizzle a little oil over them, and fold the aluminum foil over the fish, sealing the edges to keep the contents secure.

Bake for 40 minutes, then remove the foil and serve.

I buy fish at the market at Castiglione della Pescaia or Grosseto, two towns on the coast not far from Vicarello. I always make sure to buy from the stalls that sell fish brought in that very morning by local fishing boats.

SECONDO

VITELLO TONNATO
VEAL WITH TUNA DRESSING

Serves eight

3 cups white wine

1 bay leaf

Zest of ½ lemon

1 whole carrot

1 whole rib celery

1 whole onion

2½-pound cut of veal
(the veal loin eye cut is best)

Thin lemon slices for garnish

A few sprigs parsley for garnish

For the sauce

1 cup mayonnaise (page 114)

3 anchovies

30 salted capers

1 cup tuna ventresca (belly) fillets in oil,
well drained

In a saucepan, combine the wine and 1 quart of water with the bay leaf, lemon zest, carrot, celery, and onion. Bring to a boil, then place the piece of veal, whole, into the liquid. The liquid should cover it completely as it cooks; if it doesn't, add boiling water.

Return to a boil, then cover and cook over medium heat for about 90 minutes, until the meat is tender. Remove the lid and leave the veal to cool in its cooking liquid.

To make the sauce, in a mixer, beat together the mayonnaise, anchovies, half the capers, and the tuna.

When the veal has cooled, remove it from its liquid and use a very sharp knife to thinly slice it. Lay the slices on a serving dish, cover them with the mayonnaise mixture, and garnish the dish with the remaining capers, some lemon slices, and the parsley.

Cover the dish with plastic wrap and refrigerate for 4 hours before serving.

*Ventresca is the tastiest part of the tuna;
I use ventresca from Sicily . . . the very best!
Vitello Tonnato is best served straight from
the refrigerator, with a salad of lettuce
and tomatoes.*

114

CONDIMENTO

ANTIPASTO/SECONDO

MAIONESE
MAYONNAISE

Yields one cup

1 whole egg

½ cup peanut oil

½ cup extra virgin olive oil

Juice of ¼ lemon

Pinch of salt

In a tall, narrow container, combine all the ingredients. Put a handheld blender toward the bottom and work the ingredients together well without incorporating any air into the mixture until the oil and eggs have blended perfectly.

Begin to move the handheld blender up and down a little, allowing air in and thickening the mayonnaise.

For good mayonnaise, both the olive and peanut oils must be of excellent quality. For a stronger-flavored mayonnaise, use just olive oil. Freshly pressed oil will give a particularly rich flavor, and the mayonnaise will be as green as the new oil.

CARPACCIO ALLE ERBE
CURED BEEF WITH HERBS

Serves twelve

6 bay leaves, minced

Leaves from 2 sprigs rosemary, minced

20 sage leaves, minced

Leaves from 3 sprigs thyme, minced

2 cloves garlic, minced

1½ cups sea salt

Freshly ground black pepper

4-pound piece of lean beef

In a bowl, combine the herbs, garlic, salt, and pepper to taste.

Place the beef in a dish and cover it on all sides with the herb mixture. Cover with plastic wrap and leave it to marinate in the refrigerator for 3 days, turning the meat twice a day.

After 3 days, wrap the meat in butcher paper, tie it up with string, and refrigerate for at least 10 additional days.

Very thinly slice the beef and serve it with a salad.

This cured meat keeps perfectly in the refrigerator for three weeks or so.

L'ESTATE

SECONDO

CALAMARI RIPIENI
STUFFED SQUID

Serves four

20 cherry tomatoes

4 tablespoons extra virgin olive oil

4 tablespoons *passata* (page 86)

Salt

20 capers

½ pound *burrata* cheese, minced

20 small squid

Put 8 of the cherry tomatoes, 2 tablespoons of the oil, 1 tablespoon of the *passata*, and a pinch of salt in a pan and cook, covered, stirring occasionally, until the tomatoes are soft. Add 8 of the capers and the burrata.

Remove the ink sack, mouth, eyes, and bone from the squid and peel them, detaching the tentacles from the body. Wash the squid well. Chop the tentacles.

Fill each squid with the burrata mixture and close securely with a toothpick.

Put them in a pan with the remaining 2 tablespoons oil and cook over medium heat, covered, until the squid begins to soften, about 20 minutes.

Add the remaining 3 tablespoons *passata* to the pan, along with the remaining 12 cherry tomatoes, 12 capers, and the chopped tentacles, then continue cooking, covered, for about 10 minutes, until the squid is tender.

Burrata *is a buffalo-milk cheese made mostly in Italy's southern regions. The production process is identical to that of mozzarella, except that cream is injected into the center of the cheese, making it luxuriously soft and slightly runny.*

SECONDO

POLIPO IN PURGATORIO
STEWED OCTOPUS

Serves four to six

3 bay leaves, minced

Leaves from 1 bunch parsley, minced

2 cloves garlic, minced

1 chili, minced

¼ cup extra virgin olive oil

1 octopus, 2 pounds (or several smaller ones), cleaned

Sea salt

Combine the bay leaves, parsley, garlic, and chili with the oil in a large pot or earthenware casserole and cook over low heat for a couple of minutes, taking care not to let it burn.

Put the whole octopus into the casserole, season with salt, and cover tightly, placing a sheet of aluminum foil between the pot and its lid. Increase the heat to medium and continue cooking for 40 minutes, uncovering the pot occasionally (as seldom as you can) in order to make sure nothing is sticking to the bottom.

After 40 minutes, prod the octopus with a fork: if it's done, the fork will sink in easily. If it doesn't, continue cooking, adding a little water to the bottom of the pot if necessary.

Remove the octopus from the pan and serve it hot with its cooking liquid, with boiled potatoes alongside or on slices of toast.

It's easier to cook octopus that has been frozen, as the flesh gets more tender as it defrosts. Even if you buy fresh octopus, you should freeze it before using it.

SECONDO

GALANTINA DI CAMPAGNA
COUNTRY MEATLOAF

Serves six to eight

¼ pound boiled ham, diced

¼ pound Parma-style ham, diced

2 ounces veal tongue (optional), diced

½ pound chicken breast, diced

2 ounces ground pork

½ pound ground veal

2 eggs

1 cup marsala

½ cup whole pistachios

Salt and freshly ground black pepper

Combine the two kinds of ham, the tongue, and chicken breast in a bowl.

Add the pork, veal, eggs, marsala, and pistachios and season with salt and pepper, then work the mixture together well; this will take some time.

Transfer the mixture to a sheet of parchment paper and form it into a sausage shape about 3 inches thick. Wrap the parchment around it and secure it with kitchen twine. Wrap a cloth around the paper and tie it tightly with twine to keep the mixture in as it cooks.

Drop the parcel into a saucepan of slightly salted cold water, bring to a gentle boil over medium heat, and cook for 1 hour and 15 minutes.

Remove the meatloaf from the saucepan and place it on a plate to drain with a weight on top. When it has cooled completely, slice it, and place the slices on a serving dish.

You can keep this dish in the refrigerator for five or six days. It's handy to have ready for when friends turn up unexpectedly. Serve with mayonnaise (page 114) and a tomato salad.

SECONDO

SECONDO

PESCE FINTO
FAUX FISH

Serves four

1 pound potatoes, unpeeled

2 (7-ounce) cans tuna in olive oil, drained

8 anchovies in oil

1 cup mayonnaise (page 114)

20 salted capers, well rinsed

Freshly ground black pepper

2 tablespoons extra virgin olive oil

Boil the potatoes in a pot of salted water until you can push a fork into them easily. Drain them and set aside to cool.

When the potatoes have cooled, peel and mash them, and put them in a bowl with the drained tuna, 4 anchovies, ½ cup of the mayonnaise, and half of the capers. Season with pepper. Add the oil and beat well, either by hand or in a mixer on low speed, until the mixture becomes a smooth paste.

Put the mixture into a mold—a fish-shaped one is best—lined with plastic wrap, or shape it by hand and wrap it in plastic wrap.

Leave it to set for a couple of hours in the refrigerator, then turn it out onto a serving dish and garnish with the remaining capers, anchovies, and the remaining ½ cup mayonnaise.

FILETTO DI TONNO CON PESTO DI MENTA
TUNA FILLETS WITH MINT SAUCE

Serves four

1 clove garlic, peeled

Salt

Leaves from 6 sprigs mint

1 tablespoon red wine vinegar

¼ cup extra virgin olive oil

1 tuna fillet, 1½ pounds, cut into 4 pieces

Put the garlic in a mortar with a pinch of salt. Add the mint leaves and work with the pestle until a smooth paste is formed. Add the vinegar and oil.

Soak the tuna pieces in cold salted water for 15 minutes, then drain and dry them well with paper towels. Sprinkle a little salt over them and cook for 2 minutes per side on a red-hot griddle.

Serve with the mint sauce and some plain boiled new potatoes.

CONTORNO

CICORINO CON LE UOVA IN CAMICIA
CHICORY LEAVES WITH POACHED EGGS

Serves four

2 tablespoons cider vinegar

Salt

4 farm-fresh eggs

½ pound young chicory leaves, thinly sliced

5 tablespoons extra virgin olive oil

Freshly ground black pepper

Bring a low-sided saucepan filled with water to a boil. Add 1 tablespoon of the vinegar and a little salt, then lower the heat. Stir the water with a wooden spoon until the contents of the pan are moving vigorously in a clockwise direction.

Break 1 egg onto a plate, then slide it gently into the water and continue stirring in such a way that you don't touch the egg but the water swirls over the egg yolk and sets it.

After 3 minutes, remove the egg with a slotted spoon and place on a plate; repeat the process with the other eggs. Remove any foam from the egg whites with a sharp knife.

Dress the chicory with the oil and the remaining 1 tablespoon vinegar and season with salt and pepper. Divide the salad among 4 soup bowls. Place a poached egg in the center of each.

This dish, from my hometown of Milan, is rarely found anymore. The chicory I use is the bitter Cichorium intybus (dandelion chicory); the contrast between the cool, bitter salad and the hot eggs makes this simple dish a real treat.

SECONDO

PADELLATA DI UOVA AL POMODORO
PAN-COOKED EGGS WITH TOMATOES

Serves six

3 pounds ripe plum tomatoes

2 cloves garlic, unpeeled

5 tablespoons extra virgin olive oil

Leaves from 2 sprigs basil

Salt

12 farm-fresh eggs

Freshly ground black pepper

Drop the tomatoes into a pot of boiling water for 1 minute. Remove with a slotted spoon and cool slightly. Peel the tomatoes and slice them lengthwise, then remove the seeds and gently squeeze the tomatoes to remove any remaining liquid.

Crush the garlic cloves with the flat side of a knife.

Place the tomatoes in a large skillet with the oil and garlic and cook over medium-low heat for about 15 minutes, stirring occasionally. The tomatoes should not disintegrate. Add the basil leaves and season with salt. Remove the garlic.

Crack the eggs into the skillet without breaking the yolks and cook them for about 3 minutes.

Add a sprinkling of pepper, and serve the dish directly from the skillet.

This Tuscan version of a traditional dish—one of the miracles of Italian cuisine—is usually cooked by my Tuscan husband, most often for his friend Stefano R. I dedicate this recipe to the two of them.

DOLCE

DOLCE

GELATO DI CREMA
SWEET CREAM GELATO

Serves six

5 egg yolks

¾ cup sugar

Zest of 1 lemon, in strips

1½ cups milk

1½ cups heavy cream

Beat the egg yolks and the sugar until they form a pale, smooth paste.

Put the zest into the milk, bring it to the boil, and turn it off. When it has cooled a little, remove the zest, and add the cream and the beaten eggs and sugar. Mix well and return to the heat, stirring constantly until the ingredients reach a temperature of 185°F.

Plunge the pan into a bowl of ice cubes, and continue stirring until the ice cream mix is completely cold. Transfer it to the ice cream maker and churn according to the manufacturer's instructions.

GELATO DI CIOCCOLATO
CHOCOLATE GELATO

Serves six

5 egg yolks

¾ cup sugar

1½ cups milk

1½ cups heavy cream

3 ounces dark chocolate, chopped and melted in a bain-marie

In a bowl, beat the egg yolks with the sugar until they form a pale, smooth paste.

In a saucepan, heat the milk just to a boil over medium heat. Immediately turn off the heat. Cool slightly and add the cream and the beaten egg and sugar mixture.

Stir well and return to the heat, stirring constantly until the mixture reaches a temperature of 185°F. Whisk in the melted chocolate.

Plunge the pan into a bowl of ice cubes and stir until the custard mixture is cold. Transfer to an ice cream maker and churn according to the manufacturer's instructions.

DOLCE

GELATO DI NOCCIOLA
HAZELNUT GELATO

Serves six

For the hazelnut crunch

¼ cup hazelnuts

½ cup sugar

A few drops lemon juice

Almond oil for greasing the parchment

For the gelato

½ cup hazelnuts

1 tablespoon almond oil

1½ cups milk

¾ cup sugar

⅔ cup heavy cream

To make the hazelnut crunch, coarsely chop the hazelnuts with a mortar and pestle. In a small saucepan, combine the sugar, 1 tablespoon water, and the lemon juice. Place over medium heat and cook until the sugar begins to caramelize, about 3 minutes. Add the hazelnuts and continue cooking until the caramel is amber colored but not too dark; watch closely so it doesn't burn.

Turn the caramelized nuts onto a sheet of parchment paper greased with a little almond oil.

To make the gelato, in a food processor grind the hazelnuts to a fine powder; add the almond oil and process to a smooth paste.

In a saucepan, heat the milk over medium heat until it just comes to a boil. Immediately remove from the heat. Add the sugar, cream, and nut paste, and stir to dissolve the sugar and nut paste.

Plunge the pan into a bowl of ice cubes and stir until the custard mixture is cold. Transfer it to an ice cream maker, add the hazelnut crunch, and churn according to the manufacturer's instructions.

DOLCE

DOLCE

SORBETTO ALLA PESCA
PEACH SORBET

Serves six

1 cup sugar

1 pound peaches, peeled, pitted, and chopped

1 egg white

In a saucepan, combine the sugar and 1 cup water. Bring to a boil, then reduce the heat and simmer for about 10 minutes, until the sugar dissolves. Transfer the syrup to a food processor, add the peaches, and process until smooth.

Pour the mixture into a bowl and plunge into a bowl of ice cubes. Stir until the mixture is cold. Transfer to an ice cream maker and churn according to the manufacturer's instructions.

While the sorbet is churning, beat the egg white until stiff peaks form, and gradually work it into the sorbet a few minutes before you remove it from the ice cream maker. (You may not need to use all of the egg white; taste the mixture and use your judgment.)

GELATO AL LIMONE
LEMON GELATO

Serves six

1½ cups milk

¾ cup sugar

⅔ cup heavy cream

Juice of 5 lemons

Mint sprigs for garnish

In a saucepan, heat the milk over medium heat to just under a boil. Add the sugar and immediately remove from the heat. Stir until the sugar dissolves. Slowly stir in the cream and then the lemon juice.

Plunge the pan into a bowl of ice cubes and stir until the mixture is cold. Transfer to an ice cream maker and churn according to the manufacturer's instructions. Serve with mint sprigs.

I like this gelato to be not too sweet, refreshingly tart. However, if your lemons are very sour, you may wish to reduce the lemon juice by a quarter or even a half.

DOLCE

BAVARESE DI YOGURT CON PESCHE E LIME
YOGURT BAVARIAN CREAM WITH PEACHES AND LIME

Serves six

1 envelope (¼ ounce) unflavored gelatin

Almond oil or grapeseed oil, for the molds

1 lime

3 peaches, peeled, pitted, and sliced

3 tablespoons sugar

⅔ cup plain yogurt

⅔ cup heavy cream

Peach puree, for serving (optional)

In a small saucepan, stir the gelatin into a ¼ cup water. Place over low heat and stir until the gelatin dissolves and the mixture is clear. Set aside to let cool. Lightly oil six individual-size ramekins.

Grate the zest from the lime and squeeze its juice.

Place the peaches in a food processor and process to a paste; add the lime juice and zest.

Blend the gelatin mixture with the peach and lime juice mixture. Add the sugar and yogurt and whisk to dissolve the sugar.

Beat the cream until stiff peaks form, then gently fold it into the mixture.

Pour the mixture into the prepared ramekins, cover with plastic wrap, and refrigerate for at least 6 hours or overnight before serving. If you like, unmold onto plates and serve with peach puree.

This pudding can be kept in the refrigerator for several days.

DOLCE

TIRAMISÙ
TIRAMISÙ

Serves eight to ten

2 cups mascarpone cheese

5 farm-fresh eggs, separated

5 tablespoons sugar

4 espresso cups strong hot coffee

1 (7-ounce) package *pavesini* (cats' tongue) cookies

A sprinkling of cocoa powder

In a bowl, mix the mascarpone with the egg yolks and sugar. Stir to dissolve the sugar.

Beat the egg whites until stiff peaks form, then very gently using a wooden spoon, fold them into the mascarpone mixture.

Pour the coffee into a wide bowl and quickly dunk each cookie into it. Arrange about half the cookies so that they completely cover the base of a shallow (1½-inch) rectangular (11 by 7-inch) Pyrex dish, then cover them with half of the mascarpone mixture. Add another layer of dunked cookies, then the rest of the mixture, topping it off with the cocoa powder.

Cover the dish with plastic wrap and refrigerate for 4 hours before serving.

You can make a "white" version of this dessert by dunking the cookies in cold milk instead of coffee, adding chunks of seasonal fruit—peaches and strawberries are good—to the mascarpone cream, then finishing it off with a layer of fruit. Note this recipe contains uncooked eggs.

DOLCE

TORTA D'UVA
GRAPE CAKE

Serves eight

For the filling

2 pounds red grapes

1 egg

½ cup sugar, plus more for dusting

5 tablespoons extra virgin olive oil

1 cup milk

2¾ cups all-purpose flour

1 tablespoon baking powder

Preheat the oven to 375°F.

Squeeze enough grapes to yield ½ cup grape juice.

In a bowl, beat the egg with the sugar, then add the oil, milk, flour, and baking powder. Pour in the grape juice and most of the remaining whole grapes, and mix.

Line a 10-inch round cake pan with 3-inch-high sides with parchment paper, and turn the mixture into it. Dot the top with the remaining grapes and dust it with sugar.

Bake for 35 minutes, or until a toothpick stuck into the middle of the cake comes out clean. Cool the cake in the pan.

This fantastic cake symbolizes the end of summer; I make it when we're harvesting grapes for new wine. It is delicious made with Concord grapes as well.

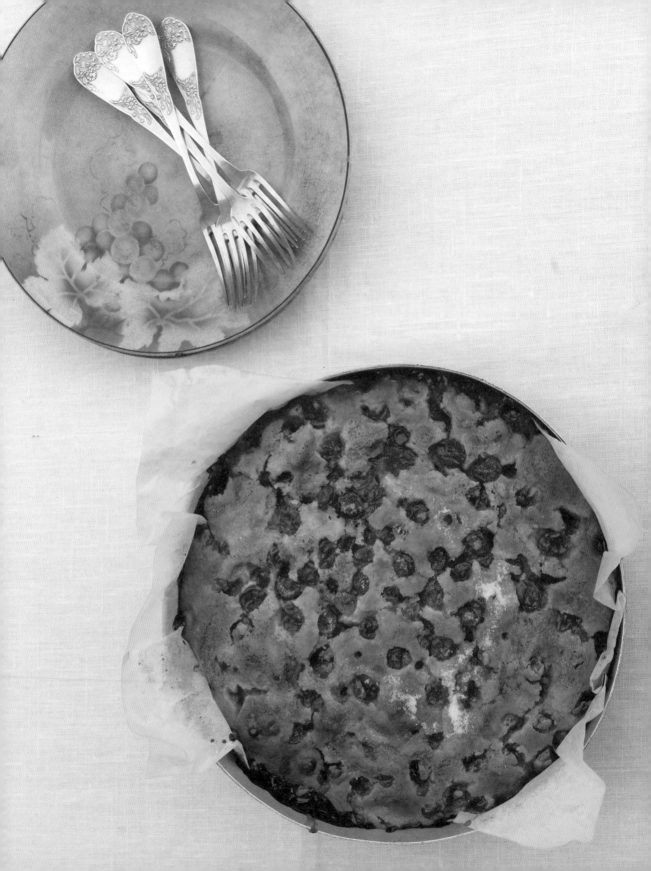

DOLCE

PESCHE ALL'AMARETTO
PEACHES WITH ALMOND COOKIES

Serves six

9 yellow peaches, peeled, cut in half, and pitted

1 egg

10 amaretti cookies, crumbled

1 tablespoon sugar

Preheat the oven to 375°F.

Cut away a little fruit from the center of 12 peach halves, enlarging the holes.

Put the peach scraps in a food processor along with the remaining 6 peach halves, the egg, and the crumbled amaretti cookies. Process until smooth with some cookie crumbs, and spoon some of each into the hole in the center of the peach halves.

Arrange the peaches in a 11 by 7-inch ovenproof dish. Dissolve the sugar in enough water—about ½ cup—to cover the bottom of the dish, and pour it in.

Bake for 30 minutes, then remove from the oven, cool completely, and refrigerate before serving.

The best-known amaretti cookies come from northern Italy and are soft. Our local amaretti cookies—made with almonds and egg whites— are crunchier and perfect for this recipe.

DOLCE

CROSTATA DI PESCHE
PEACH CUSTARD TART

Serves eight

For the pastry

2½ cups all-purpose flour

1 cup (2 sticks) butter, chilled and cut into pieces

½ cup sugar

2 egg yolks

Grated zest of 1 lemon

For the custard filling

6 amaretti cookies, crumbled

4 peaches, peeled, pitted, and thinly sliced

2 eggs, separated

⅓ cup sugar

1 tablespoon milk

To make the pastry, combine the flour, butter, sugar, egg yolks, and lemon zest in a food processor and pulse to form a smooth dough. Shape the pastry into a ball, wrap it with plastic wrap, and refrigerate for 1 hour.

Preheat the oven to 350°F and grease a low-sided 10-inch pie pan.

Roll out the pastry and line the pie plate with it.

Cover the pastry with the crumbled amaretti cookies, then cover them with the peach slices.

To make the custard filling, in a bowl, beat the egg whites until stiff peaks form. In a separate bowl, beat the yolks, sugar, and milk, then gently fold the whites into this mixture using a metal spoon.

Pour the filling over the peach slices and bake for 40 minutes, or until the crust is golden brown. Remove from the oven, cool completely, and refrigerate until ready to serve.

A variation on this tart is to make the pastry and bake it unfilled. Cool, then fill it with thick, strained yogurt that has been sweetened with sugar and folded together with whipped cream. Then top with sliced peaches or other fruit.

L'AUTUNNO

L'AUTUNNO
AUTUMN

AUTUMN IS GLORIOUS at Vicarello, as the many regular guests who venture out here from the still-sweltering cities for long languorous weekends well know.

It's a great time for wine lovers who come to tour the area's vineyards as the vines begin to take on their autumnal bronze hues. But it's a great time for total relaxation too—still sunny enough for a dip in the pool and some last-minute sunbathing during the day, but never too hot. And, as autumn progresses, it's cool enough in the evenings for the first crackling log fires.

Luckily for me, the temperature has dipped in the kitchen too, for this is the season for preserving. Figs are made into delicious jam. And they're caramelized with almonds from Vicarello's trees: I make sugar syrup and boil whole figs in it until the syrup thickens, then add the nuts and store this specialty in jars, to be eaten through the winter. The final tomatoes are removed from the plants and bottled as *passata* (page 86) for winter sauces. Or, if there are many green tomatoes that I know will not have time to ripen, I turn them into a jam, which is ideal to serve with cheese. The last of the green, yellow, and red peppers are picked and bottled, as are the eggplants. And any extra spinach is blanched briefly and squeezed into balls to be frozen.

For November 2, the *festa dei morti* (Day of the Dead), I prepare *schiaccia dei morti*—a dry bread with golden raisins and dried figs.

L'AUTUNNO
AUTUMN

IN THE GARDEN

AUTUMN IS A quiet season in the garden: it's too early to prune and too late to plant. But it's the time for reaping the benefits of all that hard work during the hot days of summer. Plants that languished in the August heat produce their final flush of glory: the roses are blooming again and the dahlias are looking splendid.

All horticultural activity is concentrated in the vegetable garden. There are the winter crops—cabbage, fennel, lettuce—to be sown. And there's fruit to be picked. The fruit trees around the vegetable garden are a battleground in autumn: Carlo and I along with the staff compete with all the neighborhood's birds for the apples and figs. But even after their raids, there's usually plenty left to eat and keep. With the last grapes that grow on a pergola near the castle, we create wonderful treats for the breakfast table, such as Torta d'Uva (page 136).

IN THE WOODS AND FIELDS

ON SUCH WONDERFUL autumn days, it's difficult to resist the lure of the countryside around the castle. But long walks through the woods and fields are productive as well as pleasurable. Cooler autumn temperatures bring almost as much new vegetable life as you find in spring.

If you know what to look for—and Carlo is an expert—there are wild spinach and beet leaves to be picked, tender dandelion florettes for dressing pasta (see page 234), and any number of wild herbs to make exquisite salads. After autumn showers, the woods are alive with mushrooms. Carlo's expertise here is not so foolproof: it's easy to identify the wonderful *funghi porcini*, but anything he's unsure about, he takes to the local mycologist to have identified before handing them over to me for cooking, in such dishes as Zuppa di Funghi (page 168).

Game is another key ingredient in the autumn kitchen, and the hunting season starts in early November. Serious hunters like Carlo, however, have a waiver, and can begin as early as August. In his hunting reserve nearer the coast at Valle di Buriano, there are pheasants, partridges, and quail, but Carlo hunts only boar, which in the kitchen at Vicarello goes into dishes such as Wild Boar Stew (see page 242)—Carlo's tour de force. The first *battuta di caccia* of the season at Buriano usually takes place late in September.

THE VINEYARD AND OLIVE GROVE
Early autumn is a busy time in the vineyard. Carlo, his staff, and all helpers he can muster—usually around eight people in all—spend three or four days bringing in the grape harvest. A few weeks later he'll fertilize the plants with organic worm compost.

As the weather gets colder, it's time to pick the olives. Again, anyone with a spare moment is welcome in the olive grove, where there are twelve hundred trees. It's a two-week job for five people. When the fruit is taken to the local press, it usually yields about six quintals—more than thirteen hundred pounds—of extra virgin olive oil: the basis of so much of what I produce in the kitchen. But this quantity, however, is far too much even for Vicarello; the remainder is sold off to the castle's most faithful guests, and to friends and acquaintances.

INSALATA D'AUTUNNO
AUTUMN SALAD

Serves four

2 rabbit legs, boned and diced

5 tablespoons extra virgin olive oil

2 tablespoons butter

10 fresh sage leaves

⅔ cup sheep's milk ricotta

1 egg plus 1 egg white

Salt and freshly ground black pepper

1 cup peanut oil

3 tablespoons all-purpose flour

½ pound small lettuce leaves

1 green apple, peeled, cored, and cubed

40 large, firm green grapes, sliced lengthwise

Seeds from 1 pomegranate

1 tablespoon balsamic vinegar

Combine the rabbit, 2 tablespoons of the olive oil, the butter, and sage in a skillet. Place over medium heat and cook, stirring occasionally, until the rabbit is cooked through, about 20 minutes. Remove from the heat and cool. Transfer to a food processor along with the ricotta, the whole egg, and salt and pepper to taste, and blend until well combined.

Heat the peanut oil in a large skillet over medium heat.

While the oil is heating, in a bowl, lightly beat the egg white. Spread the flour out over a plate.

Shape the rabbit mixture into ½-inch balls. Dip them into the egg white, then lightly roll them in the flour. Using a slotted spoon, drop the balls into the peanut oil and fry them for about 4 minutes, until golden. Transfer to paper towels to drain.

In a salad bowl, toss the lettuce with the apple, grapes, and as many of the pomegranate seeds as you like. Dress the salad with the remaining 3 tablespoons olive oil and the vinegar. Serve the salad with the fried meatballs.

TARTELLETTE DI SPINACI
INDIVIDUAL SPINACH PIES

Serves four

For the pastry

⅓ cup all-purpose flour

1½ cups whole wheat flour

⅓ cup extra virgin olive oil

Juice of 1 lemon

Salt

For the filling

1¼ pounds fresh spinach

10 salted capers

4 olives, pitted

1 anchovy

Leaves from 1 sprig thyme

5 ounces *crescenza* cheese (see Note, page 96) or any soft, creamy cheese

To make the pastry, combine the two types of flour in a food processor with the oil, lemon juice, and pinch of salt. With the machine running, slowly add about ⅓ cup cold water and process until a smooth dough is formed. Wrap the dough in plastic wrap and refrigerate for 1 hour.

Grease and flour 4 individual 4-inch pie pans. Roll out the dough and cut it into shapes slightly larger than the pie pans. Line the dishes with the pastry, allowing it to hang over the edges.

Preheat the oven to 375°F.

Blanch the spinach in a pot of boiling water until wilted. Drain and squeeze it well to remove the water. Finely chop the spinach.

Mince together the capers, olives, anchovy, and thyme to make a smooth paste, and toss the spinach with it.

Put a layer of spinach in each pie pan, cover it with *crescenza* cheese, then fold the overhanging pastry back over the filling. Bake for 30 minutes.

This recipe was a chance invention. One day, some friends turned up unexpectedly and I made a meal with whatever I could find around the kitchen. This was what I came up with.

PATÉ DI CASA MIA
HOMEMADE PÂTÉ

Serves eight to twelve

2 pounds veal livers

¾ pound chicken livers

2 cloves garlic

10 tablespoons butter

3 bay leaves

Salt and freshly ground white pepper

¾ cup cognac

1 cup dry white wine

Meat Stock (page 164), as needed

¾ cup heavy cream

Remove the thin membranes from the veal livers, then thinly slice the livers. Wash the chicken livers well to remove the excess fat, then dice. Crush the garlic cloves with the flat side of a knife. Place the veal and chicken livers in a pot with 1 stick butter, the bay leaves, and garlic; season with salt and white pepper. Cook over high heat for 5 minutes, stirring, then pour in the cognac and white wine.

Continue cooking until all the liquid has evaporated, stirring with a wooden spoon to keep the liver from sticking to the bottom. Add a ladle of stock—two, if necessary—and simmer for 4 minutes, until a sauce forms.

Remove the bay leaves and garlic and pass the mixture through a food mill or blend it to make a sauce. Return the sauce to the pot and cook over low heat for 2 to 3 minutes, stirring constantly with a wooden spoon.

In a separate saucepan, melt the remaining butter with the cream. Remove the liver sauce from the heat and stir in the butter and cream, mixing thoroughly.

Butter a pâté mold (or line it with plastic wrap), pour the mixture in, and cool. Cover the surface with plastic wrap and refrigerate for 24 hours.

At my family home we would make this pâté every Christmas to eat during the festive season. You can serve it with toasted country-style bread.

PANINI RIPIENI
FILLED ROLLS

Serves six

3 potatoes

½ pound ham in thick slices, diced

5 ounces salami, diced

½ pound mixed cheeses (such as provolone, Emmental, pecorino, Parmigiano-Reggiano), diced

½ cup grated Grana Padano cheese

Salt and freshly ground black pepper

1 envelope (2¼ teaspoons) active dry yeast

4 cups all-purpose flour

1 cup plus 2 tablespoons milk

3 eggs

⅓ cup extra virgin olive oil

In a large bowl, dissolve the yeast in 1 cup of room-temperature water. Add ¾ cup of the flour and leave the mixture to rise for about 1 hour, until bubbles form on top.

Boil the potatoes in a pot of water until tender, then drain and mash them. Cool.

In a bowl, combine the ham, salami, mixed cheeses, and grana cheese, and season with salt and pepper to taste.

Add the rest of the flour, 1 cup of the milk, 1 teaspoon salt, the eggs, and mashed potatoes and work the ingredients into a soft dough.

Roll the dough out into a rectangle about ¼ inch thick. Spread the meat and cheese filling over the top, then roll the dough around the filling like a jelly roll, beginning from a wide side. Cut the roll into 2½-inch-wide slices and smooth the dough over the sliced edges to seal the filling inside and form them into dough balls. All the filling should be covered up by dough.

Grease a 10-inch cake pan and sprinkle it with flour. Arrange the dough balls in the pan and leave them to rise for 2 to 3 hours, until they double in size and touch each other, forming a sort of lumpy pie.

Preheat the oven to 375°F. Brush the "pie" with the remaining 2 tablespoons milk and bake for 40 minutes, or until golden brown.

To serve this very attractive form of "lumpy" focaccia, place it on a large serving plate in the middle of the table so that everyone can tear off the piece they like. It's an extremely social dish!

CROSTINI DI FEGATINI
CHICKEN LIVER ON TOAST

Serves eight

1 onion, minced

½ cup (1 stick) butter

3 bay leaves

12 chicken livers, cleaned and each cut into 4 pieces

1 cup dry white wine

3 tablespoons Meat Stock (page 164), or as needed

6 anchovies

2 tablespoons salted capers, well rinsed

8 slices toasted country-style bread for serving

Combine the onion with 5 tablespoons of the butter and the bay leaves. Place over medium heat, and when it begins to take on color, add the livers and cook for 5 minutes, stirring, until they begin to turn golden. Add the wine, stir until it evaporates, then add the stock, scraping the bottom of the pot with a wooden spoon to release any of the livers that have stuck.

Remove the livers from the heat, cool, and mince with the anchovies and capers. Return it to the pot with the remaining butter and cook for a couple of minutes, stirring constantly. Don't let it come to a boil.

Drizzle the toast with stock and spread the livers over the toast.

This dish is totally Tuscan. The cooked livers keep well for several days stored in an airtight container in the refrigerator.

INSALATA DI RADICCHIO E NOCI
RADICCHIO AND WALNUT SALAD

Serves four

1 pound red Treviso radicchio, leaves torn in half

1½ cups walnuts, shelled

½ pound fontina cheese, diced

3 tablespoons extra virgin olive oil

2 teaspoons Dijon mustard

Salt

Combine the radicchio, walnuts, and fontina in a salad bowl.

In a small bowl, whisk together the oil, mustard, and a little salt until the mixture is emulsified. Toss the salad with the dressing.

Salads are an important part of our spring and summer diet at Vicarello, and we're so fond of them that we can't do without in the colder months either. I like to add cheese and nuts to make them more hearty and filling.

ANTIPASTO

ALICI FRESCHE CON L'UVA
FRESH ANCHOVIES WITH GRAPES

Serves six to eight

½ pound fresh anchovies, boned

Salt

Zest and juice of 1 lemon

Leaves from 1 sprig lemon thyme, minced

2 tablespoons extra virgin olive oil

Ground allspice

1 bunch white grapes, cut in half lengthwise

Toasted bread for serving

Lay the anchovies out in a dish with a little salt, the lemon juice, thyme, and oil. Refrigerate for 20 minutes.

Remove the anchovies from the refrigerator and add the lemon zest, pinch of allspice, and grapes. Serve with slices of toasted bread.

At Vicarello, with our abundance of meat and game, we don't eat much fish during the autumn and winter. Anchovies, however, are the exception to this rule—we eat these healthful fish year-round.

PRIMO

VELLUTA DI ZUCCA E ZENZERO
CREAM OF PUMPKIN AND GINGER SOUP

Serves six

1 clove garlic

3 tablespoons extra virgin olive oil

1 chili, thinly sliced

1 pound pumpkin, peeled, seeded, and diced

1 2-inch piece ginger, grated

6 cups Vegetable Stock (see page 222)

Salt and freshly ground black pepper

Croutons for serving

Crush the garlic clove with the flat side of a knife.

In a large saucepan, heat the oil with the garlic and chili over medium heat. When it begins to sizzle, add the pumpkin and ginger and toss for a few seconds. Remove the garlic, then add enough stock to cover the vegetables. Season with salt and pepper, and bring to a boil. Reduce the heat and cook for 20 minutes, until the pumpkin is soft, adding more stock if necessary.

Remove from the heat, transfer to a blender, and blend until smooth. Serve hot with croutons.

This dish is also excellent if you substitute one third of the pumpkin with two zucchini and omit the ginger (add the zucchini along with the pumpkin). Serve with a drizzle of olive oil and grated Parmigiano-Reggiano.

PRIMO

GNUDI DI RICOTTA E ZUCCA
RICOTTA AND PUMPKIN GNOCCHI

Serves six

1 pound ricotta

1 pound pumpkin, peeled, cut in half, seeds removed, and sliced 1 inch thick

1 egg yolk

Salt and freshly ground white pepper

All-purpose flour

2 tablespoons butter

12 leaves from several sprigs sage

2 amaretti cookies, crumbled

In a sieve lined with cheesecloth, drain the ricotta overnight in the refrigerator. You should then have about 1¼ cups thick ricotta.

Preheat the oven to 375°F.

Wrap the pumpkin slices in aluminum foil and place on a baking sheet. Place in the oven and bake for 1 hour. Check with a toothpick or fork to see that they're cooked through. Remove from the oven, cool, then pass them through a food mill or work them in a blender until smooth.

Transfer to a bowl and add the ricotta, egg yolk, and salt and pepper to taste. Stir until smooth, then, with well-floured hands, form tablespoon-size scoops into balls. If the dough is too wet, fold in just enough flour—about a tablespoon—until it comes together more easily.

Dip the balls in flour and drop them into a pot of boiling salted water. When they bob to the surface, they're ready; remove them carefully with a slotted spoon. In a skillet, melt the butter with the sage. Serve the gnocchi with the sage butter and a dusting of crumbled amaretti cookies.

This ricotta-based dumpling is an alternative to traditional pasta, without the pasta envelope used for ravioli or tortelli—hence the Italian name, which means "naked." For this recipe you want a pumpkin or winter squash that has dense and rather dry flesh.

CONDIMENTO

PRIMO

BRODO DI CARNE
MEAT STOCK

Yields about six cups

1 whole carrot

1 whole rib celery

1 whole onion

1 bunch parsley

1 bunch basil

2 chicken wings

1 veal bone with muscle attached

1 veal rib

Salt

Combine all the ingredients except the salt in a large saucepan with 3 quarts water. Place over medium-high heat and bring to a boil, skimming any foam from the surface. Reduce the heat and simmer for 2 hours. Season with salt to taste while the stock is still warm.

Strain the stock through a sieve and leave it to cool completely, then remove the layer of fat that forms on top. If you're making this in summer, you'll need to refrigerate it for the layer of fat to form.

Like my vegetable stock (page 222), this stock can be poured into ice cube trays and frozen into cubes.

STRACCIATELLA
BROTH WITH EGG

Serves four to six

4 eggs

6 tablespoons grated Parmigiano-Reggiano

2 tablespoons breadcrumbs

Freshly grated nutmeg

2 tablespoons finely chopped parsley

Salt

6 cups Meat Stock (opposite)

In a bowl, beat the eggs with the Parmigiano-Reggiano, breadcrumbs, pinch of nutmeg, parsley, and salt to taste.

In a saucepan, bring the stock to a boil, then pour in the egg mixture, beating constantly with a whisk for about 5 minutes. Serve piping hot.

This is a very old recipe, which is rarely made these days. But it's simple and delicious—it's time for a comeback!

PRIMO

PASTA E FAGIOLI CON LE COZZE
BEAN AND PASTA SOUP WITH MUSSELS

Serves six

2 pounds mussels in their shells, cleaned

¾ pound dried cannellini beans

2 cloves garlic, unpeeled

Leaves from 1 sprig sage

4 tablespoons extra virgin olive oil

2 tablespoons *passata* (page 86)

¼ pound fresh *tagliolini* pasta, uncooked

Chopped parsley leaves for garnish

In an earthenware casserole, combine the beans, 1 clove garlic, a few sage leaves, and 2 tablespoons of the oil. Add 2 quarts water, place over medium-high heat, and bring to a boil. Reduce the heat and simmer for about 2 hours, until the beans are soft. Drain the beans, reserving the cooking water, discard the garlic, and pass the beans through a food mill or puree them in a blender.

Heat a large skillet over medium-high heat. Add the mussels to the skillet, cover, and cook, shaking the skillet from time to time until the shells open and the mussels release their liquid, about 5 minutes. Set the mussels and their juice aside, discarding any mussels that do not open.

Crush the garlic cloves with the flat side of a knife.

Return the casserole used for the beans to the stovetop and add the remaining 2 tablespoons oil, the *passata*, the remaining garlic clove, and the remaining sage leaves. Cook for about 5 minutes, then add the pureed beans with a little of their cooking water. Strain the liquid from the mussels through a strainer lined with cheesecloth to remove any sand. Remove the garlic, add the mussel liquid to the soup, then add the tagliolini. Fresh pasta will take about 3 minutes to cook to al dente, dry pasta from a package about 10 minutes.

Remove the mussels from their shells and, 1 minute before the pasta is cooked, add them to the pot. Serve hot, garnished with the parsley.

The addition of mussels enhances this traditional country fare. Tagliolini are a thinner-shaped version of tagliatelle, which you may substitute here if needed.

PRIMO

ZUPPA DI FUNGHI
MUSHROOM SOUP

Serves four to six

1½ pounds porcini mushrooms
or mixed wild mushrooms

¼ cup parsley leaves

1 clove garlic

4 cups Vegetable Stock (page 222)

⅓ cup all-purpose flour

2 tablespoons butter

6 tablespoons extra virgin olive oil

Salt and freshly ground black pepper

1 slice country-style bread, cut into cubes

Preheat the oven to 400°F.

Remove the stems from the mushrooms. Chop and reserve them. Thinly slice the caps.

Mince the parsley and garlic together.

Bring the stock to a boil in a saucepan, then turn off the heat, cover, and set aside.

Spread the flour over an ovenproof dish, put it in the oven, and toast the flour for about 5 minutes, until it turns very pale golden. Pour the flour into the stock, whizz it with a handheld blender, and cook for 7 minutes, stirring occasionally.

In a large skillet, melt the butter in 4 tablespoons of the oil until it begins to foam, then add the minced garlic and parsley, and the mushroom pieces—first the stalks and, after a couple of minutes, the caps. Cook until the mushrooms begin to release their liquid, 6 to 7 minutes, then season with salt and pepper and remove from the heat.

Add the cooked mushrooms to the stock and simmer for 30 minutes.

Heat the remaining 2 tablespoons oil in a skillet over medium heat. Add the bread cubes and toss until golden. Serve the soup sprinkled with the croutons.

PRIMO

ZUPPA DI PICCIONE RIFATTA
LEFTOVER SQUAB SOUP

Serves six

1 ounce pancetta, minced

3 tablespoons extra virgin olive oil

1 carrot, minced

1 rib celery, minced

1 onion, minced

1 squab, stewed according to recipe on page 176, plus the gravy and bones

6 cups hot Meat Stock (page 164)

Salt and freshly ground black pepper

6 slices country-style bread, toasted

Grated Parmigiano-Reggiano for serving

Put the pancetta and oil in an earthenware pot. Place over low heat and cook for 3 minutes, then add the carrot, celery, and onion. Continue cooking over low heat for 10 minutes, making sure the vegetables don't brown.

Add the squab meat, gravy, and bones and stir with a wooden spoon until it's very hot, then add the stock. Season with salt and pepper and simmer for about 90 minutes.

Remove the squab from the pot. Remove the bones, scraping off any flesh left attached, and add it to the soup.

Place a slice of bread at the bottom of each soup bowl and ladle the soup over it. Sprinkle with grated Parmigiano-Reggiano.

Although this wonderful soup is made from leftovers from Stewed Squab (page 176), it's so good that you might be tempted to cook the squab from scratch just to make the soup.

PRIMO

TORTELLI DI FAGIANO AL BURRO E ROSMARINO
PHEASANT TORTELLI WITH BUTTER AND ROSEMARY

Serves six

1 young pheasant

2 tablespoons extra virgin olive oil

2 ounces pancetta, minced

2 shallots, minced

1 cup dry white wine

2 tablespoons grated Parmigiano-Reggiano

1 egg

¾ cup heavy cream

Salt and freshly ground black pepper

Tortelli Dough (page 38)

3 tablespoons butter

Leaves from 1 sprig rosemary, minced

Preheat the oven to 375°F. Bone the pheasant and remove the drumsticks. Cut off the breast.

Heat a large ovenproof dish on the stovetop over medium-high heat. When it is very hot, add the oil. Add the pheasant drumsticks and breasts, placing the breasts skin side down. Cook without stirring until the pheasant turns a golden color.

Add the pancetta and shallots, turn the pheasant, and continue cooking for another minute or two. Add the wine and allow it to evaporate, stirring.

Transfer the dish to the oven and cook until the meat is done: the flesh inside should be pink and the outside should not be dried out; cooking times vary depending on the bird. Remove from the oven, cool slightly, then transfer to a food processor, discarding any bones, and blend to a smooth paste.

In a large bowl, combine the pheasant mixture, the Parmigiano-Reggiano, egg, and cream, and season with salt and pepper to taste. Mix well, cover, and refrigerate for 1 hour.

Roll out the tortelli dough and cut into circles of about 2 inches in diameter. You want about 30 tortelli, 5 per person. Place 2 teaspoons of filling on 30 pasta circles, then cover with 30 more pasta circles. Crimp edges with a fork to seal. Bring a large pot of salted water to a boil and cook the tortelli for about 8 minutes, until they float to the surface. Drain.

In a small skillet, melt the butter with rosemary over low heat and pour it over the tortelli.

The recipe for this filling was given to me by two dear friends from London, Emily and Connor, who are both keen pheasant hunters. The recipe was a joint collaboration, as I taught them how to make the fresh pasta.

SECONDO

STINCO DI VITELLO ALLA BIRRA
BEER-BAKED VEAL SHANK

Serves six to eight

2 cloves garlic

Leaves from 1 sprig sage

3 tablespoons butter, slightly softened

2 teaspoons Aromatic Salt (page 46)

1 medium veal shank

Salt and freshly ground black pepper

3 tablespoons extra virgin olive oil

2 cups lager

Preheat the oven to 375°F.

Coarsely chop the garlic and sage together. Take a good-size lump of butter and mix it with the aromatic salt and garlic and sage mixture.

Use a small, sharp knife to make incisions in the veal shank and fill them with the butter mixture.

Season the veal with salt and pepper and place it in a large saucepan with the remaining butter and the oil. Place over medium heat and cook, turning regularly until it turns golden all over, then transfer to the oven and bake for 30 minutes, turning it after 15 minutes.

Turn the meat again and cover the pot. Turn again after 15 minutes; after 30 minutes add the beer, then remove the cover and continue cooking and turning, basting with the juice from time to time. The meat is done when it begins to come away from the bone, about 2½ hours. Let the meat rest for a few minutes, then carve it along the bone and serve, passing the gravy separately.

This dish was a favorite of my father's; he would make it with almost maniacal care, and it would always fill the house with wonderful aromas. Serve with Potatoes Baked with Thyme (page 254) or mashed potatoes.

SECONDO

PICCIONI IN CASSERUOLA, OVVERO PICCIONI ALLA LUISA
STEWED SQUAB

Serves four

2 squabs, each about 1 pound

2 tablespoons butter

2 cloves garlic, peeled

9 slices pancetta

½ teaspoon Aromatic Salt (page 46)

2 tablespoons extra virgin olive oil

½ cup dry white wine

Meat Stock (page 164), as needed

Clean the squabs, pass them through a flame to remove any remaining feathers, and stuff each with 1½ teaspoons of butter, 1 garlic clove, half a slice of pancetta, and ¼ teaspoon aromatic salt.

Wrap 4 slices of pancetta around each squab breast and tie the squab with twine, then place them in a saucepan with the remaining 1 tablespoon butter and the oil. Cook over low heat, turning them until they are uniformly golden brown.

Raise the heat, pour the wine over the squab, and allow the wine to evaporate completely.

Add a ladle of stock, cover the saucepan, lower the heat, and cook for about 40 minutes, turning the squab after 20 minutes and adding more stock if the liquid is drying out, until they are cooked through.

This is one of my mother's recipes. It is excellent served with mashed potatoes.

SECONDO

SPIEDINI
MEAT SKEWERS

Serves four

2 to 3 slices stale country-style bread,
cut into 1-inch cubes

¾ pound pork shoulder, cut into large cubes

¾ pound fresh pork belly, cut into large cubes

1 red pepper, cut into large cubes

4 sausages, each cut into thirds

Bay leaves

Extra virgin olive oil

White wine

Preheat the oven to 375°F.

Skewer the ingredients, starting with a piece of bread, which will hold the rest on safely. After the bread, add a piece of pork shoulder, followed by pork belly, pepper, sausage, a bay leaf, and more bread, and repeat the sequence until each skewer is full. You will make 8 skewers.

In a small bottle, pour in 1 inch each of olive oil, wine, and water and shake well.

Place the skewers in an ovenproof dish, drizzle them with the oil mixture, and bake for 40 minutes, turning them after 15 and 30 minutes.

These skewers are great alongside barbecued meats; serve with a simple green salad.

CONDIMENTO

SECONDO

CONDIMENTO PER CARNE ALLA GRIGLIA
BARBECUE SEASONING

Yields about one-half cup

2 tablespoons dark brown sugar

¾ cup grappa

1 teaspoon freshly ground black pepper

2 tablespoons finely chopped rosemary leaves

1 tablespoon large-grain salt

2 tablespoons extra virgin olive oil

Mix the ingredients together and use to season meat.

CARNE DI MAIALE ALLA GRIGLIA
GRILLED PORK

Serves ten

8 pork ribs

10 slices fresh pork belly

8 pork cutlets

8 sausages

Barbecue Seasoning (opposite)

A few hours before you're ready to serve, prepare a barbecue using large quantities of the most fragrant types of wood available; at Vicarello this would include juniper, bay, and rosemary.

Prepare the meats by sprinkling them with the seasoning.

When the fire has died down and you are left with a pile of very hot embers, place the meat on a grill over the embers; there should be no flames. Cook the ribs for just 4 minutes and the other meats for 15 minutes or more, turning the meats the moment they become golden brown. There's no need to add oil.

SECONDO

GRAN BOLLITO
MIXED BRAISED MEATS

Serves six

3 whole carrots

1 whole rib celery

1 whole medium onion

3 whole cloves

1 clove garlic

1 bunch parsley

5 black peppercorns

Sea salt

1-pound piece brisket

1-pound piece veal chuck steak

1 veal tail, 1½ pounds

1 veal tongue, 1½ pounds

Fill a large saucepan with 2½ quarts (10 cups) water; add the carrots, celery, onion, cloves, garlic, parsley, peppercorns, and 1 tablespoon salt, and bring to a boil.

Add all the meat, reduce the heat to medium-low, cover, and simmer until the meat is cooked through and a fork slides easily into the flesh, 2 to 3 hours.

The key to success with this wonderful traditional recipe is to put the meat into the water when it's boiling fast. The ratio of salt to water is also vital. You can vary the recipe by adding a chicken, but it must be free-range; a pig's trotter is also a good option, though it should be cooked separately from the rest of the meat.

Serve with your choice of Green Sauce (page 184), chutneys, horseradish, and/or Spicy Tomato Sauce (page 184).

CONDIMENTO

SALSA VERDE PER CARNI E PATATE LESSE
GREEN SAUCE FOR MEAT AND BOILED POTATOES

Yields one and one-half cups

2 tablespoons white wine vinegar

1 bread roll

8 capers, well rinsed

1 cup minced parsley leaves

1 hard-boiled egg, peeled

⅓ cup extra virgin olive oil

In a bowl, combine the vinegar with ¼ cup water. Remove the crust from the roll and soak the soft insides in the vinegar. Discard the crust.

Squeeze out the bread and put it in a blender or food processor. Add the remaining ingredients and blend to make a creamy paste.

Salsa verde will keep for several days in the refrigerator.

CONDIMENTO

SALSA DI POMODORO SPEZIATA
SPICED TOMATO SAUCE

Yields four cups

4 cups *passata* (page 86)

3 tablespoons sugar

5 tablespoons white wine vinegar

1 chili (optional)

1 cinnamon stick

2 whole cloves

1 teaspoon salt

Combine all the ingredients in a saucepan and bring to a boil over medium-high heat. Reduce the heat and simmer for 1 hour. Remove the cinnamon and cloves and blend until smooth.

SECONDO

STINCO DI MAIALE ALLE MELE
PORK BRAISED WITH APPLES

Serves four

Leaves from 1 sprig rosemary

Leaves from 1 sprig sage

1 clove garlic

Salt

2 tablespoons butter, softened

2 pork shanks

3 tablespoons extra virgin olive oil

3 tablespoons grappa

Meat Stock (page 164), as needed, about 1 cup

2 cooking apples, cored and halved

Mince the rosemary, sage, and garlic together. Beat some salt into the butter and add the herbs and garlic. Make 3 or 4 incisions in each shank and fill them with some of the butter.

In a casserole, melt the remaining butter in the oil over low heat and cook the shanks, turning them frequently until they become golden brown all over. Raise the heat, pour in the grappa, and let it evaporate completely. Add a ladle of stock, reduce the heat to low, and cook until the meat is tender, about 1½ to 2 hours, stirring occasionally and adding a little more stock if the bottom of the pot starts to get dry. Add the apples about five minutes before the meat is done.

If you like, instead of adding the apples, you can serve the shanks with applesauce. For a final touch, serve with Prunes Wrapped in Pancetta (page 188).

SECONDO

PICCIONI CON I FICHI
SQUAB WITH FIGS

Serves four

2 squabs, about 1 pound each

4 slices pancetta

2 bay leaves

2 cloves garlic

10 black figs

4 tablespoons extra virgin olive oil

2 tablespoons butter

¼ cup brandy

Meat Stock (page 164), as needed

⅔ cup heavy cream

Clean the squabs and, if necessary, pass them over a flame to remove any last bits of feather. Wrap the breasts with 1 slice pancetta each, securing with kitchen twine. Stuff each squab with 1 slice pancetta, 1 bay leaf, 1 garlic clove, and 1 or 2 figs, depending on how big they are.

Heat the oil and butter in a casserole over medium heat. Add the squabs and cook until they begin to turn golden. Add the brandy and cook until the liquid evaporates. Reduce the heat to low, cover the pan, and cook, turning the squabs every 15 minutes or so and scraping the pan to prevent sticking, until the squabs are golden brown outside and the flesh inside feels tender when tested with a toothpick, about 40 minutes. If it starts to dry out, add a ladle of stock from time to time.

When the birds are almost ready, add the cream and stir for a few minutes, then remove the squabs and tent with foil to keep them warm. Put the remaining figs in the pot and cook over low heat for a couple of minutes to warm through. Return the squabs to the pot and stir.

Serve half a squab to each diner, with the figs and cooking liquid.

CONTORNO/ANTIPASTO

PRUGNE AVVOLTE NELLA PANCETTA
PRUNES WRAPPED IN PANCETTA

Serves six

12 pitted prunes

2 fresh pork sausages (optional), crumbled

12 strips pancetta (or bacon)

Preheat the oven to 400°F.

Fill the hole in each prune with sausage meat, if using. Wrap 1 strip of pancetta around each prune. Place them seam-side down in an ovenproof dish and bake for 10 minutes, or until the pancetta is crisp.

SECONDO

ARROSTO DI VITELLO CON SALSA ALLE NOCI
ROAST VEAL WITH WALNUT SAUCE

Serves six

2 pounds tender veal for roasting (silverside heel is best)

2 tablespoons butter

2 tablespoons extra virgin olive oil

1 cup Meat Stock (page 164), warmed

1½ cups walnuts

⅓ cup heavy cream (optional)

Preheat the oven to 375°F.

Tie the veal with kitchen twine so it keeps its shape while roasting.

In a casserole on the stovetop, melt the butter in the oil over medium-high heat. Place the veal in it and brown it well all over. Add the stock, cover, and place in the oven. Bake for about 1½ hours, until it is cooked through: when the meat is done, no blood will appear when you pierce it with a skewer.

Remove from the oven and set aside, keeping the veal covered and warm.

Process the walnuts to a powder in a food processor. Add them, along with the cream, if using, to the juices in the casserole and cook over low heat on the stovetop for 5 minutes. Slice the veal and serve it with the nut sauce drizzled over the top.

Adding cream will make the walnut sauce thicker and richer, though the dish is equally good without it.

DOLCE

CANTUCCI
ALMOND BISCOTTI

Yields about four dozen

1½ cups almonds

4 cups all-purpose flour

1½ cups sugar

3 whole eggs plus 2 egg yolks

1 teaspoon baking powder

Salt

Preheat the oven to 375°F and line a baking sheet with parchment.

Toast the almonds for a few minutes in a nonstick pan over medium heat. Remove from the heat and cool.

Place the flour in a bowl and make a well in the center. In the well, put the sugar, 2 of the whole eggs, the egg yolks, baking powder, and a pinch of salt. Gradually fold the flour into the other ingredients, adding the almonds halfway through.

Knead the dough until the ingredients come together, dusting your hands with flour so the mixture doesn't stick.

Shape the dough into loaves about 2 inches wide and ½ inch high. Place them far apart on the baking sheet and brush them all over with a beaten egg. Place in the oven and bake for about 30 minutes, until golden on top but still soft. Transfer the loaves to a cutting board. While they're still hot, slice them diagonally ½ inch thick and leave the *cantucci* to harden as they cool on a rack.

These hard, dry biscotti—wonderful after dinner dipped into a good dessert wine—originated in the Tuscan town of Prato but are now served all over the world. They'll keep well for weeks in an airtight container. Unlike other similar biscotti you may know, these cookies are baked just once, not twice.

DOLCE

TORTA AL CIOCCOLATO DI NERI
NERI'S CHOCOLATE CAKE

Serves eight

7 ounces dark chocolate, chopped

1 cup (2 sticks) butter

1 cup sugar

1½ cups all-purpose flour

1 tablespoon baking powder

½ cup milk

3 eggs, separated

Preheat the oven to 375°F and grease a 9-inch round baking pan.

Melt the chocolate and butter with the sugar in a double boiler or in a heatproof bowl placed over a pan of simmering water. Transfer to a bowl and add the flour, baking powder, milk, and egg yolks. Mix well.

In a separate bowl, beat the egg whites until stiff peaks form, then gently fold them into the chocolate mixture.

Pour the mixture into the prepared cake pan and bake for 35 minutes, or until a toothpick inserted in the center comes out clean. Leave the cake to cool in the pan, then turn onto a plate to serve.

This recipe is dedicated to my son Neri, who must have eaten hundreds of these cakes over the years. He is also very good at making it. For something different, the cake can be made with ricotta cheese in place of the butter: melt the chocolate with the sugar, then add ¾ cup ricotta; proceed with the recipe as written.

DOLCE

CROSTATA DI RICOTTA CON MARMELLATA DI ARANCE
RICOTTA TART WITH BITTER ORANGE MARMALADE

Serves six

For the pastry

3 eggs

2 cups all-purpose flour

½ cup sugar

Grated zest of 1 lemon

½ cup (1 stick) butter, chilled and cut into pieces

For the filling

2 cups ricotta

¾ cup sugar

2 eggs, separated

Zest of 1 lemon

Zest of 1 orange

Cinnamon

Bitter orange marmalade

To make the pastry, boil the eggs in a pot of water for 7 minutes. Drain, cool, then peel them and separate the yolks from the whites. Save the whites for another use.

Place the flour and sugar in a food processor; add the lemon zest, butter, and boiled egg yolks, and process until the dough comes together. Place the dough between two sheets of parchment paper and roll it out about ⅛ inch thick. Line the bottom of an 11-inch tart pan with the dough, trimming it to fit. Refrigerate for 1 hour.

Preheat the oven to 375°F.

To make the filling, in a bowl, combine the ricotta, sugar, egg yolks, the lemon and orange zests, and a pinch of cinnamon.

Beat the egg whites until soft peaks form, then fold them into the ricotta mixture and spread the filling over the pastry. Bake for about 40 minutes, until the crust is golden.

Leave to cool in the dish, then slide it onto a plate to serve. Either spread the marmalade over the top of the tart or serve it on the side.

DOLCE

SEMIFREDDO CON SALSA AL CIOCCOLATO FONDENTE
SEMIFREDDO WITH DARK CHOCOLATE SAUCE

Serves six

For the semifreddo

5 egg yolks

5 heaping tablespoons sugar

2 cups heavy cream

For the chocolate sauce

6 ounces dark chocolate, finely chopped

½ cup whole milk

1 cup heavy cream

In a large bowl, beat the egg yolks with the sugar. Whip the cream until stiff peaks form and fold it into the yolks.

Line a 9 by 5-inch loaf pan with parchment paper, pour the mixture into it, cover with plastic wrap, and freeze for 4 hours to make the semifreddo.

Place the chocolate in a heatproof bowl. In a saucepan, bring the milk and cream just to a boil. Remove from the heat and pour over the chocolate. Stir until the chocolate melts.

Remove the semifreddo from the freezer and slice it ½ inch thick. Serve drizzled with the chocolate sauce. (The sauce can be served either hot or cold; be aware that it thickens considerably as it cools.)

Semifreddo is made with much the same ingredients as ice cream, but it is denser because it isn't churned in an ice cream machine.

DOLCE

BISCOTTI ALLE NOCCIOLE
HAZELNUT COOKIES

Yields about twenty-five cookies

2½ cups all-purpose flour

1½ teaspoons baking powder

6 tablespoons butter, softened

¼ cup sugar

¼ cup milk

1 egg white, beaten

¼ cup hazelnuts, coarsely chopped

Preheat the oven to 375°F and line a baking sheet with parchment.

Sift the flour and baking powder into a mixer and add the butter, sugar, and milk. Mix to form a smooth dough.

With well-floured hands, shape the dough into 1-inch balls. Place the balls on the baking sheet with an inch or two between them and press them down flat. Brush them with the beaten egg white and sprinkle with the hazelnut pieces.

Bake for about 15 minutes, until the cookies are golden; they will still be soft when you take them out of the oven but will harden as they cool.

DOLCE

FRITTELLE DI RISO
RICE FRITTERS

Yields about thirty fritters

4 cups milk

Zest of 2 lemons

Salt

1 cup rice, uncooked

4 tablespoons (½ stick) butter

½ cup granulated sugar

1½ cup golden raisins

2 eggs, separated

1 teaspoon baking soda

¾ cup all-purpose flour

2 tablespoons rum

4 cups peanut oil

⅓ cup confectioners' sugar

In a saucepan, bring the milk to a boil with half the lemon zest and a pinch of salt. Add the rice and boil for 5 minutes, then add the butter and granulated sugar. Cook for about 5 minutes, stirring, until the milk is completely absorbed. Remove from the heat, transfer to a bowl, then cover and refrigerate overnight.

The following morning, soak the golden raisins in warm water for 5 minutes, drain them and pat dry with paper towels, then add them to the rice mixture. Add the egg yolks, baking soda, flour, rum, and the remaining lemon zest.

Beat the egg whites until stiff peaks form. Gently fold them into the rice and mix well.

Heat the oil in a wok or large skillet over high heat. When it is very hot (but not smoking), drop in teaspoonfuls of the rice mixture and fry for about 2 minutes, until golden. Remove with a slotted spoon, drain on paper towels, and roll them in the confectioners' sugar.

It pays to make lots of these fritters. Somehow there never seem to be enough!

DOLCE

PRUGNE CON LE NOCI E CREMA AL CIOCCOLATO
PRUNES WITH WALNUTS AND CHOCOLATE CREAM

Yields thirty stuffed prunes

4 ounces dark chocolate, broken into pieces

½ cup heavy cream

1½ tablespoons butter, softened

30 pitted prunes

30 walnut halves

Place the chocolate in a heatproof bowl. In a small saucepan, bring the cream just to a boil, add the butter, and pour this over the chocolate pieces. Stir until the butter and chocolate have melted, and the mixture is smooth.

Fill a larger bowl with ice cubes and place the bowl with the chocolate cream into the ice, beating with a whisk to cool it quickly and make a thick cream; this will take about 5 minutes.

Cover the bowl and refrigerate for about 3 hours to fully set.

Spoon the cream into an icing bag and pipe it into the holes in the pitted prunes. Close the top of each hole with a walnut half.

These stuffed prunes will keep for several days refrigerated in an airtight container.

DOLCE

CROSTATA DI FICHI E PERE
FIG AND PEAR TART

Serves six to eight

For the pastry

1¼ cups all-purpose flour

1¼ cups semolina flour

½ cup sugar

¾ cup (1½ sticks) butter, chilled and cut into pieces

3 egg yolks

For the filling

10 fresh or dried figs

4 tablespoons (½ stick) butter

½ cup sugar

4 firm Bartlett pears, peeled, quartered, and cored

To make the pastry, place the two flours and the sugar in a food processor and pulse to combine. Add the butter and egg yolks and pulse to form a ball. Wrap the pastry in plastic wrap and refrigerate for 1 hour.

Preheat the oven to 375°F and line a 10-inch tart pan with parchment paper.

For the filling, if you are using dried figs, soak them in a bowl of hot water for 2 minutes to soften. In a nonstick skillet, melt the butter with the sugar over medium heat. Arrange the pears with their outsides facing downward in the pan. Add the figs and cook, covered, for 5 minutes, then uncover the skillet and continue cooking until slightly caramelized, about 5 minutes.

Transfer the fruit to the prepared tart pan, arranging the pears and figs artfully. Set aside to cool.

Roll the pastry out to a ¼-inch thickness, place it over the fruit, and seal the edges.

Bake for about 35 minutes, until the crust is golden. Cool on a wire rack, then invert onto a serving dish with the fruit on top.

There are two types of figs: those that ripen in the late spring and those that are ready to pick for all of September and early October. We have one tree in particular that keeps us very busy making jams and preserves for several weeks.

DOLCE

BUDINO DI RISO
BAKED RICE PUDDING

Serves six

½ cup golden raisins

2 tablespoons all-purpose flour

4 cups milk

1½ cups Arborio rice, uncooked

Zest of 1 lemon

Salt

3 eggs, separated

⅔ cup sugar

Preheat the oven to 375°F and grease and flour a muffin pan or one 10-inch cake pan.

Soak the golden raisins in cold water for 5 minutes. Drain them, dry with paper towels, and roll them in the flour.

In a saucepan, combine the milk with 2 cups water. Add the rice, lemon zest, and a pinch of salt, and bring to a boil. Reduce the heat and continue cooking until almost all the liquid has been absorbed, about 5 minutes; the remainder will be absorbed as the rice cools.

In a bowl, beat the egg yolks with the sugar. Beat the egg whites until stiff peaks form.

When the rice has cooled to room temperature, mix in the egg yolk mixture. Add the golden raisins, then carefully fold in the egg whites using a stainless steel spoon, moving the mixture from the bottom upward.

Turn the rice mixture into the pan(s) and bake for 35 minutes for the individual pans, 50 minutes for the large pan. The surface of the pudding will be slightly browned when ready. Leave the pudding in the pan(s) to cool and turn out to serve.

This baked rice pudding can also be made with a thin pastry case covering it. If you'd like to make it that way, use the pastry from the Peach Custard Tart recipe (page 140) and cover the rice mixture before baking. Bake for about 5 minutes longer, until the pastry is golden. For the rice, I use the round soup rice called Originale. *You can substitute any type of short-grain rice.*

PANE

PANINI AL MIELE
HONEY ROLLS

Yields ten rolls

1⅓ cups milk, at room temperature

1 envelope (2¼ teaspoons) active dry yeast

¼ cup honey

4 cups all-purpose flour

Salt

Beaten egg or milk for brushing the rolls

Combine the milk and yeast in the bowl of a mixer and set aside for a few minutes to dissolve. Add the honey, flour, and a pinch of salt and, using the dough hook, mix until a smooth dough forms. Cover the bowl with a dish towel and leave the dough to rise until it doubles in size, about 1 hour.

Press down on the dough without removing too much air from it, then divide it into 10 balls. Place the balls on a baking sheet lined with parchment paper. Leave to rise for 1 hour.

Preheat the oven to 400°F.

Brush the rolls with beaten egg or milk, and bake for about 25 minutes, until the tops are golden brown. Remove from the oven and transfer the rolls to a rack to cool.

These rolls are excellent for breakfast or served with cured meats.

FOCACCIA DI PATATE
POTATO FOCACCIA

Serves six

1 envelope (2¼ teaspoons) active dry yeast

1 tablespoon sugar

2½ cups all-purpose flour

2½ cups semolina flour

1 teaspoon salt

½ cup extra virgin olive oil, plus more for brushing

4 small potatoes, peeled and chopped

Combine the yeast and sugar with 1⅔ cups room-temperature water, and set aside for 10 minutes to dissolve. Add the two types of flour, the salt, and oil to the bowl of a mixer and, using the dough hook, mix until a smooth dough forms. Set aside to rise until doubled in size, about 90 minutes.

Boil the potatoes in a pot of water until tender, then drain and mash them. Cool.

Mix the mashed potatoes into the dough, knead well, and spread the dough out onto a greased baking sheet.

Leave the dough to rise for 40 minutes.

While the dough is rising, preheat the oven to 475°F.

Place the focaccia in the oven and bake for about 40 minutes, until golden brown. Brush generous amounts of olive oil over the top and serve.

This is especially delicious if you top the focaccia with a handful of cherry tomatoes and pitted black olives before putting it in the oven. When making focaccia or any other bread product, don't allow the yeast to come directly in contact with the salt, as salt can hamper the leavening properties of the yeast. You always want yeast to be dissolved in a liquid or mixed with flour first.

PANE/ANTIPASTO/SECONDO

PIZZA
PIZZA

Serves four

1 teaspoon active dry yeast

2½ cups all-purpose flour

Salt

1 clove garlic

1 cup canned peeled tomatoes

2 tablespoons extra virgin olive oil

Leaves from 2 sprigs basil, chopped,
or 5 pinches dried oregano

¼ pound mozzarella, thinly sliced

Dissolve the yeast in a bowl with ¼ cup room-temperature water, then add ½ cup of the flour. Mix well, cover, and let stand for about 8 hours.

Add the remaining 2 cups flour, ½ cup water, and a pinch of salt, and work well to form a smooth dough. Cover with a dish towel and let rise for an hour or two, until it doubles in size.

While the dough is rising, crush the garlic clove with the flat side of a knife. Dress the tomatoes with the garlic, oil, and basil; season with salt. Mash the tomatoes with a fork and set aside to marinate for 1 hour. Remove the garlic before using.

Preheat the oven to 550°F and lightly oil a baking sheet.

The best way to prepare the pizza dough is by hand: Flatten the ball of dough, then begin pulling it gently outward from the edges, leaving a thicker ring around the outside. Place the disc on the prepared baking sheet, spread the tomato mixture on top, and bake for 15 minutes.

Add the mozzarella slices, return to the oven, and bake for another couple of minutes, until the cheese is melted. Remove from the oven and serve immediately.

For the best results, you will need to prepare the dough many hours before: in the evening for the following day's lunch, or in the morning for that day's dinner.

L'INVERNO

L'INVERNO
WINTER

WINTER AT VICARELLO is a time to take stock and make plans for the coming year. Three months after the harvest, when the first frosts have caused the leaves to fall, it's time to prune the vines. With about six acres of vineyards to tend to around the *castello*, Carlo and his assistants spend four to five painstaking weeks cutting back each plant by hand. The clippings are shredded and returned to the soil around the vines; everything about production here is organic and biodynamic. Meanwhile, the current year's harvest has gone through its fermentation process and is ready to be transferred to the French oak casks, where it will be left to age. Grape must, the seeds and skins that remain after the juice is pressed, is being transformed into grappa—the clear, fiery liquor that Italians love as a *digestivo* after a meal.

This is the season for reaping the benefit of all that boiling and bottling activity that seemed so tiresome in the summer heat. There are preserves and jams to spread on homemade bread, eat with cheese, or make into *crostate* (jam tarts); there's bottled fruit, and *passata di pomodoro*, that essential tomato base for so many recipes. This is also the season to start enjoying the dried fruit and nuts that feature so prominently on the Christmas table.

Aromatic oils and salts concocted now can be used for the rest of the year. I add dried herbs like bay, sage, and rosemary to bottles of the current year's new oil, along with dried chili and sea salt; you can vary the mixture with peppercorns, dried parsley, and dried thyme. The longer you leave it, the better it tastes; let it stand for at least one month and keep plenty for dressing summer salads. Salt, too, is excellent flavored with the addition of fennel seeds, crushed dried herbs, and chili.

L'INVERNO
WINTER

IN THE GARDEN

THE COLD WEATHER may have arrived, but the vegetable garden
is far from dormant. Sheltered from the northerly winds, my *orto* still
has some salad crops—*cappuccio* (butterhead) and *rouge d'hiver* (a
French romaine) lettuces, purple-red radicchio, and hardy *scarola*
(escarole). Dark green *cavolo nero* (black kale) is another winter treat.
Bulbous, blanched globes of fennel were first produced in Tuscany in
the seventeenth century from the wild plant, and it's still an important
ingredient in the winter kitchen. Leeks and carrots, celeriac, and
turnips go into warming soups; and there's still parsley and rosemary
for flavoring. In the more sheltered corners, wild strawberries are
still bearing fruit, hidden beneath leaves that are gradually turning a
burnished gold. More threatening to the *orto* than cold in this season are
the animals that are finding it harder to forage in the open: *caprioli* (roe
deer) will nibble leaves off neatly but exhaustively; *cinghiali* (boar) and
istrici (porcupines) delve and destroy as they devour leaves and roots.

HUNTING

ON CARLO'S THOUSAND-ACRE Valle di Buriano reserve, near the
coastal town of Castiglione della Pescaia, the hunting season is in full
swing. Four *battute* (hunts) are organized each year in this wild expanse
of Mediterranean *macchia*, cork, and holm oaks. Although *cervi* (red
deer), *daini* (fallow deer), and *fagiani* (pheasants) abound here, only one
species is actually hunted: the *cinghiale*, or wild boar, which reproduces
at an alarming rate. On the hunt day, the fifteen *cacciatori*—the men
wearing an obligatory shirt and tie beneath their green or brown oilskin
jackets—take up position on the wooden *palchette*, or "stages," that have
been set up at strategic points, while the *canai*, or dog-handlers, send
out their charges to encircle the prey. The master blows a horn, and the
three-hour hunt begins.

Though it has its opponents, hunting is one of those Tuscan traditions
(like mushroom picking or chestnut gathering) that links people to the
land; it's as rooted in the territory as the Sangiovese grape and far more

ancient. Wild boar, hare, pheasant, and guinea fowl find their way into so many Tuscan dishes; and as the locals well know, wild specimens are always superior to farm-bred varieties.

CHRISTMAS TRADITIONS

As in most of Italy, Christmas is generally a quiet time at Vicarello, dedicated to family and friends, who gather in the castle's focal point—the kitchen—and help out with the preparation of *pasticci* (pâtés), stuffed dried fruits (see page 263), or Italy's favorite Christmas sweet treat, the spongy *panettone*. The woods, fields, and orchards provide materials for seasonal table decorations. Pyramids of bay leaves, studded with oranges or lemons (which, when the decorations are taken down on Twelfth Night, are turned into marmalade). Cypress cones and *corbezzolo* (strawberry tree) berries add a splash of rustic color.

ANTIPASTO

PERE AL CARAMELLO CON ROBIOLA O CAPRINO
CARAMELIZED PEARS WITH *ROBIOLA* CHEESE

Serves four

1 teaspoon mustard powder

1 teaspoon yellow mustard seeds

¾ cup sugar

2 tablespoons honey

1 cinnamon stick

2 pears, peeled, cored,
and quartered lengthwise

⅓ cup *robiola* or another soft, creamy cheese

Pour 2 cups water in a saucepan. Whisk in the mustard powder, mustard seeds, sugar, and honey. Add the cinnamon. Bring to a boil and boil until reduced slightly. Add the pear quarters, reduce the heat, and simmer, covered, for 5 minutes. Remove the cover and simmer for an additional 10 minutes, or until the liquid thickens to a syrup.

Arrange the warm pear quarters on plates, with a spoonful of the cheese beside them. Serve with the syrup drizzled on top.

CONDIMENTO

BRODO VEGETALE
VEGETABLE STOCK

Yields about six cups

2 tablespoons extra virgin olive oil

1 carrot, roughly chopped

1 rib celery, roughly chopped

1 leek, roughly chopped

1 onion, roughly chopped

½ cup dry white wine

1 clove garlic

1 bunch herbs
(thyme, rosemary, marjoram, or parsley)

Salt

Heat the oil in a saucepan over low heat and add the vegetables. Sauté them for about 5 minutes. Add the wine and cook, stirring, until it evaporates, then add 2 quarts water, the garlic, herbs, and salt to taste. Simmer for 30 minutes, then strain.

This stock can be frozen in ice cube trays and used whenever you need just a small amount of stock.

ANTIPASTO/CONTORNO

INSALATA DI RUCOLA E MELOGRANO
ARUGULA SALAD WITH POMEGRANATE

Serves four

4 cups arugula leaves

Seeds from ½ pomegranate

2 tablespoons extra virgin olive oil

1 teaspoon balsamic vinegar

Salt and freshly ground black pepper

2-ounce piece Parmigiano-Reggiano, shaved into slivers

In a large salad bowl, combine the arugula and pomegranate seeds. Add the oil and vinegar and toss to coat. Season with salt and pepper. Divide the mixture among plates and sprinkle the Parmigiano-Reggiano over the top.

This recipe works equally well without balsamic vinegar—if you don't have very high-quality balsamic, it's best to omit it.

CROSTONI DI CANNELLINI E CAVOLO NERO
CANNELLINI BEANS AND BLACK KALE ON TOAST

Serves four to six

4 cloves garlic, unpeeled

1 medium onion, chopped

1 cup dried cannellini beans

10 leaves sage

8 peppercorns

¼ cup extra virgin olive oil,
plus more for drizzling

1 whole chili

1 bunch black kale,
stems removed, thinly sliced

2 cups Vegetable Stock (page 222)

Salt

4 to 6 thick slices country-style bread, toasted

Crush 2 of the garlic cloves with the flat side of a knife, peel them, and place them in an earthenware pot along with the onion, beans, sage, and peppercorns. Cover completely with cold water and bring just to a boil. Reduce the heat and simmer for 2 to 3 hours, until the beans are cooked through; don't let the water boil.

In a large sauté pan, heat the oil over low heat. Add the chili and the 2 remaining cloves of garlic, taking care not to let them burn. Add the kale and sauté for 10 minutes. Remove the garlic and chili.

Drain the cooked beans, remove the garlic, and add the beans to the kale along with the stock. Season with salt to taste. Cook over low heat for 20 minutes, or until the mixture has become a thick soup with very little liquid.

Place a slice of bread in each soup bowl, ladle the soup over it, and serve drizzled with a little oil.

The beans can be soaked overnight to speed things up, but cooking them the same day in this way works fine.

INSALATA DI ARANCE E OLIVE NERE
ORANGE AND BLACK OLIVE SALAD

Serves four

4 oranges, peeled, pith removed, and sliced

2 ounces black olives, pitted

3 tablespoons extra virgin olive oil

Salt and freshly ground black pepper

Arrange the orange slices on a serving plate and sprinkle the olives on top.

In a small bowl, whisk the oil with salt and pepper, then pour the dressing over the oranges. Set aside for 5 minutes before serving.

This salad is also excellent with thinly sliced fennel added to it.

INSALATA DI PUNTARELLE
ASPARAGUS CHICORY SALAD

Serves four

1 head asparagus chicory (*catalogna*)

1 clove garlic

2 tablespoons anchovy paste

3 tablespoons extra virgin olive oil

½ teaspoon red wine vinegar

Remove the darker green parts of the leaves from the asparagus chicory and cut the stalks and paler parts into very thin lengthwise strips. Soak them in a bowl of water filled with ice cubes for 2 hours. The strips should curl up.

Rub the inside of a salad bowl with the garlic. In a small bowl, beat the anchovy paste with the oil and vinegar until they form a smooth dressing. In the salad bowl, dress the asparagus chicory with the dressing.

Sometimes called Italian dandelion or catalogna, asparagus chicory has long, thin serrated leaves with white ribs down the middle and, at the heart, crunchy new shoots. The flavor is distinctively bitter. If you can't find asparagus chicory, try making this salad with minced endive, celery, or fennel.

PRIMO

ACQUACOTTA
"COOKED WATER" SOUP

Serves six

¼ cup extra virgin olive oil

1 large onion, coarsely chopped

½ chili

Leaves from 1 bunch of celery, coarsely chopped

Leaves from 1 bunch parsley, coarsely chopped

1 pound spinach leaves

2 handfuls basil leaves, coarsely chopped

1 pound ripe, peeled tomatoes

Salt and freshly ground black pepper

6 slices slightly stale country-style bread

6 eggs

Grated Parmigiano-Reggiano for serving

In a nonstick skillet, heat the oil over low heat. Add the onion and chili and sauté until the onion turns golden. Add the celery, parsley, spinach, and basil leaves and sauté until the ingredients begin to turn a darker color.

Add the tomatoes, mashing them slightly with a fork. Season with salt and pepper. Continue to cook over low heat for about 2 hours, adding enough water to cover the ingredients and topping the water up halfway through. The soup should not be too liquid when it's finished.

Place a slice of bread in a bowl for each person, and pour a generous helping of broth over it. While the broth is still steaming hot, break an egg into each bowl, then sprinkle with Parmigiano-Reggiano.

Thin slices of toast can be substituted for the country-style bread. Instead of whole eggs, you can also beat three eggs and add them to the broth while it's still in the pan, then serve; leave the pan on the stove for five minutes if you prefer your eggs a little firmer. If fresh, ripe tomatoes are not available, use canned ones. As with all simple dishes, it's important that you use the very best ingredients and the greatest care for the best results.

PRIMO

ZUPPA DI LENTICCHIE E FUNGHI PORCINI
LENTIL AND PORCINI SOUP

Serves four to six

¾ ounce dried porcini mushrooms

2 cloves garlic, unpeeled

¼ cup extra virgin olive oil

1 small onion

1 chili

1 thick slice pancetta (optional), diced

3 tablespoons *passata* (page 86)

1½ cups small brown lentils

Salt

Soak the mushrooms in a bowl of warm water for 5 minutes, then drain, reserving the liquid, and set aside. Crush the garlic cloves with the flat side of a knife.

Heat the oil in a large skillet over medium heat. Add the garlic, onion, chili, and pancetta, if using. When the onion begins to turn golden, add the *passata* and cook, stirring, for 5 minutes. Add the lentils and cook for 30 seconds more. Add 6 cups water and season with salt. Bring to a boil, then turn down the heat, cover the pan, and simmer until the lentils are tender and there is little liquid left: how long this takes will depend on the lentils you use—tasty little brown lentils from Onano in Lazio take about 40 minutes. You may need to add some water as it cooks if the lentils start to dry out.

Remove the garlic, add the mushrooms and their liquid if needed into the soup, and serve.

This soup is excellent served in bowls of Whole-Wheat Pastry Made with Olive Oil (page 232).

PASTA INTEGRALE ALL'OLIO DI OLIVA
WHOLE-WHEAT PASTRY BOWLS

Serves six

1½ cups whole wheat flour

½ cup all-purpose flour

1 chili (optional), minced

1 tablespoon extra virgin olive oil

Preheat the oven to 350°F.

Place all the ingredients in the bowl of a mixer. Begin beating, gradually adding water (about ½ cup) until a ball forms. Wrap the pastry in plastic wrap and refrigerate for 1 hour.

Form 6 balls of aluminum foil about the same diameter as a small soup bowl. Divide the pastry into 6 pieces and roll them out thinly until they are large enough to drape over the foil balls to form "bowls." Place them on a baking sheet and bake for about 30 minutes, until crisp. Discard the foil and serve while still hot, filled with soup, such as Lentil and Porcini Soup (page 230).

CREMA DI CARDI
CREAM OF CARDOON SOUP

Serves four

2 pounds cardoons

1 lemon, cut in half

6 cups Meat Stock (page 164) or Vegetable Stock (page 222)

4 eggs

Salt

¼ cup aged pecorino

Freshly ground black pepper

Croutons for serving

Remove the stringy filaments from the cardoon sticks with a sharp knife or potato peeler. Rub the cardoons with lemon to keep them from turning black.

Cut the cardoon sticks into 2-inch lengths, then simmer them in a pot of water for about 1 hour, until a fork can pierce them easily. Drain them and puree in a food processor. Strain the pulp to remove any remaining filaments.

In a saucepan, bring the stock to a boil and add the cardoons.

Beat the eggs with a pinch of salt and the pecorino; season with pepper. Remove the soup from the heat, add the egg mixture, and return the saucepan to the stove, stirring constantly until it comes to a boil. Spoon into bowls and serve with croutons.

I've given this recipe to many British friends who were familiar with cardoons by sight but had no idea what to do with them in the kitchen. Hopefully they're now becoming a very popular ingredient there!

PRIMO

SPAGHETTI AL DENTE DI LEONE
SPAGHETTI WITH DANDELION LEAVES

Serves six

Salt

1 pound dandelion leaves

3 cloves garlic, unpeeled

5 tablespoons extra virgin olive oil

½ chili

1 bay leaf

5 black peppercorns

1 sprig rosemary

1 sprig sage

1 pound spaghetti

Bring a pot of salted water to a boil and add the dandelion leaves. Bring back to a boil, then reduce the heat and simmer for about 20 minutes. Drain and set aside to cool.

Crush the garlic cloves with the flat side of a knife. Heat the oil in a large skillet over medium-high heat. Add the garlic, chili, bay leaf, peppercorns, rosemary, and sage. When the oil is very hot, remove the herbs, peppercorns, and garlic and add the dandelion leaves. Season with salt and cook for 10 minutes, tossing constantly with two wooden spoons. Use kitchen scissors to cut the leaves up a little.

Bring a pot of salted water to a boil and cook the spaghetti until al dente. Drain it and add to the dandelion leaves, tossing over high heat for a couple of minutes.

Any leftovers can be kept and made into a tortino *the next day: heat some olive oil in a skillet and cook the dressed pasta until crisp on both sides. The day-old pasta should hold together on its own.*

PRIMO

RISOTTO AL RADICCHIO ROSSO DI TREVISO
RISOTTO WITH RED RADICCHIO

Serves four

2 tablespoons extra virgin olive oil

½ pound radicchio, sliced into thin strips

Salt

½ cup dry white wine

3 tablespoons butter

1 medium onion, minced

1 cup risotto rice (Vialone Nano is best)

4 cups Vegetable Stock (page 222), heated

1 clove garlic, minced

1 tablespoon minced parsley leaves

Freshly ground black pepper

¼ cup grated Grana Padano cheese

Heat the oil in a large skillet, add the radicchio and a pinch of salt, and place over medium heat. Cook, covered, for 5 minutes. Remove the cover and continue cooking until the liquid has evaporated. Add the wine and cook, stirring, until it evaporates.

In a high-sided skillet, melt 1 tablespoon of the butter over medium heat. Add the onion and sauté until softened, then add the rice and cook for 1 minute, stirring constantly with a wooden spoon. Add the radicchio and 2 ladles of stock and cook, stirring frequently and adding more stock each time the rice has absorbed almost all the liquid.

Five minutes before the rice is done, add the garlic and parsley and season with salt and pepper to taste.

The risotto is ready when the rice is still slightly hard in the center: cooking times vary enormously depending on what kind of rice you use. Remove from the heat and add the remaining 2 tablespoons butter and the grated Grana Padano.

The two kinds of red radicchio used by Italian chefs are radicchio di Verona, *which is round with tightly interlaced leaves, and* radicchio di Treviso (or trevigiano), *with longer, more open heads of garnet red leaves.*

CIME DI RAPA SALTATE IN PADELLA
PAN-TOSSED TURNIP GREENS

Serves four to six

2 pounds turnip greens

Salt

2 cloves garlic, unpeeled

½ chili

5 tablespoons extra virgin olive oil

Clean the greens, discarding everything except the most tender leaves and shoots.

Bring a large saucepan of salted water to a boil, add the greens, and boil them for 10 minutes. Drain, reserving the cooking water.

Crush the garlic cloves with the flat side of a knife and place them in a skillet, along with the chili and oil. Place over medium heat and sauté for 2 minutes. Add the greens and toss them in the oil for 10 minutes, adding a little of the greens cooking water if they show any sign of drying out or sticking to the bottom. Season with salt to taste and remove the garlic before serving.

This makes an excellent side dish for lamb or roast pork. For a more filling dish, you can add pork sausages to the greens while you're tossing them in the oil. Broccoli rabe may be substituted for the turnip greens.

FOCACCIA UMBRA CON RIPIENO DI CIME DI RAPA
UMBRIAN FOCACCIA WITH TURNIP-GREENS FILLING

Serves six

1 envelope (2¼ teaspoons) active dry yeast

½ cup extra virgin olive oil

1 tablespoon grated sharp pecorino or Parmigiano-Reggiano

4¾ cups all-purpose flour

Sprinkle the yeast over ¼ cup lukewarm water and let rest until dissolved, about 5 minutes. Combine the yeast mixture with all the other ingredients along with about 2½ cups water in a mixer and mix with the dough hook for about 2 minutes to make a smooth dough. Roll out to a ¾-inch thickness.

Preheat a cast-iron griddle for about 15 minutes. Do not use a skillet; the pizza must be cooked on a flat surface. Add the pizza dough and cook for about 15 minutes per side, until it is golden brown.

Cut the pizza into wedges, then slice each horizontally and fill with Pan-Tossed Turnip Greens (opposite) or other cooked green vegetables.

Unlike other focaccia recipes, this one does not call for letting the dough rise. Serve with a selection of fresh and aged pecorino.

SECONDO

ARISTA CON RIPIENO DI PRUGNE
RACK OF PORK STUFFED WITH PRUNES

Serves six

2-pound rack of pork with backbone

15 pitted prunes

1 clove garlic, thinly sliced

A few sage leaves

A few rosemary leaves

Salt and freshly ground black pepper

2 tablespoons butter

¼ cup extra virgin olive oil

3 tablespoons cognac

2 cups milk

Ask your butcher to open the rack of pork out flat, leaving the backbone in.

Soak the prunes in a bowl of warm water for 5 minutes; drain.

Insert the garlic slices, prunes, and sage and rosemary leaves between the meat and the bone. Season with salt and pepper. Roll up the rack and tie it tightly with twine.

Melt the butter in the oil in a large saucepan over low heat. Place the rack of pork in the saucepan and brown it on all sides. Sprinkle it with the cognac, raise the heat to medium, and continue cooking until the alcohol has evaporated.

Warm the milk in a small saucepan, then add it to the pork and simmer over medium-low heat until the rack is cooked through, at least 1 hour. Add more milk if the pan begins to dry out. Rest briefly, then slice and serve with the hot juices from the saucepan.

SECONDO

SCOTTIGLIA DI CINGHIALE
WILD BOAR STEW

Serves four to six

⅓ cup extra virgin olive oil

1 clove garlic plus 2 cloves garlic, minced

2 pounds wild boar meat, diced

3 bay leaves

Leaves from 1 sprig rosemary, minced

Leaves from 2 sprigs sage, minced

6 juniper berries

1 cup dry white wine

2 cups *passata* (page 86)

Salt and freshly ground black pepper

About 6 cups Meat Stock (page 164)

Crush the whole garlic clove with the flat side of a knife. Place 1 tablespoon of the oil in a large skillet and add the crushed garlic. Place over medium-high heat and add the boar meat. If any liquid is released from the meat, remove it with a spoon.

When the meat has more or less stopped losing liquid (how long this takes will vary considerably depending on the meat you use), add the remaining oil, the minced garlic, bay leaves, rosemary, sage, and juniper berries. Mix well and cook for 20 minutes.

Add the wine, let it evaporate, then add the *passata* and continue stirring. Season with salt and pepper and add 1 cup of stock.

Reduce the heat, cover the skillet, and cook until the meat is tender, about 3 hours, depending on the meat, adding stock as needed to keep the liquid from drying out. Serve with steaming Cornmeal Polenta (page 254).

This recipe can be used with any mixture of meats, including chicken, pork, and lamb. If the meat is store-bought, it's unlikely that you'll need to wait until liquid appears. Take care to add each type of meat depending on the length of time it takes to cook: the slowest-cooking type should go in first, followed in turn by the others, so that all are ready to eat at the same time. My husband, Carlo, is a maestro at this recipe: he once cooked it at the Four Seasons Hotel in New York for 150 guests!

SECONDO

POLLO ALLA CACCIATORA
HUNTER'S-STYLE CHICKEN

Serves six

1 free-range chicken, about 3½ pounds

1 clove garlic

¼ cup extra virgin olive oil

1 onion, thinly sliced

1 rib celery, thinly sliced

Leaves from 2 sprigs parsley, minced

Leaves from 1 sprig rosemary, minced

Salt and freshly ground black pepper

1 bay leaf

½ cup dry white wine

1 cup *passata* (page 86)

Cut the chicken into individual serving pieces. Crush the garlic clove with the flat side of a knife, peel it, and place it in a large skillet along with the oil. Place over low heat, add the onion, celery, parsley, and rosemary, and cook for 10 minutes, or until the onion is golden. Add the chicken pieces and season with salt and pepper. Cook for about 20 minutes, turning frequently, until browned. Remove the garlic.

Crumble the bay leaf, add it to the pan, and cook for 1 minute. Pour in the wine, raise the heat, and stir until it evaporates.

Add the *passata* and reduce the heat to low. Cover the pan and cook until the meat is tender (about 30 minutes for a supermarket chicken; as much as 2 hours for a free-range one).

For something different, you can add porcini mushrooms to this dish: Soak one and three-quarter ounces of dried mushrooms in warm water for one hour, and add to the chicken in place of the bay leaf.

This dish pairs well with Sweet and Sour Pickled Onions (page 254) or mashed potatoes.

CIPOLLINE IN AGRODOLCE
SWEET AND SOUR PICKLED ONIONS

Serves six

1 pound small onions, preferably cipolline

1 tablespoon sugar

1 cup white wine vinegar

1 cup extra virgin olive oil

½ teaspoon salt

Peel and wash the onions and put them in a saucepan with the remaining ingredients and 1 cup water. Place over low heat, bring to a simmer, and simmer until the onions are soft enough to push the point of a knife into but not falling apart.

These pickled onions go well with boiled or roast veal. They keep well in the refrigerator for up to one week.

TORTINO DI CAVOLFIORE ALLA MAREMMANA
MAREMMAN-STYLE CAULIFLOWER

Serves four

Salt

1 large head cauliflower

All-purpose flour for dredging

¼ cup extra virgin olive oil

3 tablespoons *passata* (page 86)

4 eggs

Freshly ground black pepper

Bring a large saucepan of salted water to a boil. Add the cauliflower head and boil for about 8 minutes, until it is slightly softened at the center, then drain it and pat dry with paper towels. Cut into florets and dip them in flour. Shake off any excess flour and set the pieces aside.

Heat the oil in a nonstick skillet over medium heat, add the cauliflower florets, and sauté until they are golden. Add the *passata* and cook for a few minutes more. Break the eggs into the pan and cook for 2 minutes on top of the cauliflower.

Season with salt and pepper and serve piping hot.

This is another recipe given to me by the women of our nearest village. It's cucina povera *(peasant cooking) in the extreme—and at its finest.*

SECONDO

VALIGETTE DI CAVOLO VERZA
SAVOY CABBAGE PARCELS

Serves four to six

24 large savoy cabbage leaves

Salt

1 pound ground veal

¼ pound ground sausage

2 eggs

2 tablespoons crumbled pieces of semi-stale bread, soaked in ⅓ cup milk

2 tablespoons grated Grana Padano cheese

Leaves from 1 sprig parsley, minced

Freshly ground black pepper

2 tablespoons butter

3 tablespoons extra virgin olive oil

1 medium onion, minced

1 slice pancetta, minced

½ cup dry white wine

Nutmeg

Slice away part of the tough central rib from each cabbage leaf, taking care not to damage it. This will make the leaves easier to fold.

Bring a large pot of salted water to a boil. Add the cabbage leaves, reduce the heat, and cook about 3 minutes, until wilted. Drain the leaves carefully and place them in a single layer on a clean dish towel to dry.

To make the stuffing, combine the veal with the sausage, eggs, soaked breadcrumbs, Grana Padano, and parsley. Season with salt and pepper and leave the stuffing to stand for 1 hour.

Place pairs of cabbage leaves together to make 12 double layers, then place an equal amount of the stuffing in the center of each. Roll the leaves up into 12 parcels and tie them with kitchen twine.

Melt the butter in the oil in a large skillet over medium heat. Add the onion and pancetta, and cook until the onion is golden. Place the cabbage parcels in the skillet and cook, turning them gently, until the cabbage leaves are a pale golden brown on all sides. Add the wine, raise the heat, and continue cooking for 20 minutes, adding water if the liquid dries out. Season with salt and pepper and a grating of nutmeg.

Serve with Stewed Cannellini Beans (page 255), mashed potatoes, or a simple salad dressed with extra virgin olive oil.

SECONDO

FARAONA ALL'ARANCIA
GUINEA FOWL WITH ORANGE

Serves six

2 organic oranges

½ cup sugar

2 tablespoons butter

1 tablespoon extra virgin olive oil

2 shallots, minced

1 guinea fowl, about 3 pounds,
cut into individual pieces

Salt and freshly ground black pepper

1 tablespoon Grand Marnier

1 tablespoon white wine vinegar

2 bay leaves

2 whole cloves

Remove the peel of 1 orange with a vegetable peeler and cut it into matchsticks. Bring a small saucepan of water to a boil, immerse the orange peel in the water, and boil for 2 minutes. Drain.

In the same pan, combine the sugar with 1 cup water and bring it to a boil, stirring to dissolve the sugar. Add the orange peel and boil for 10 minutes. Drain and set aside.

Melt the butter in the oil in a casserole over low heat. Add the shallots and sauté for 1 minute, then add the guinea fowl pieces. Continue cooking until the pieces become golden brown, turning often. Season with salt and pepper.

Squeeze the juice from both of the oranges and pour it into the casserole; add the pieces of orange peel, the Grand Marnier, vinegar, bay leaves, and cloves. Partially cover the casserole, leaving a crack for steam to escape, and cook over low heat for about 40 minutes, adding a little water if the casserole begins to dry out. When it's done, the meat will be tender and lightly browned on the outside.

Arrange the guinea fowl on a serving dish and drizzle with the cooking liquid.

Serve with Lamb's Lettuce Salad with Orange Dressing (page 255) and Potatoes Baked with Thyme (page 254).

SECONDO

COSTOLE DI VITELLO IN CASSERUOLA CON FUNGHI PORCINI
STEWED VEAL CHOPS WITH PORCINI

Serves four to six

1½ ounces dried porcini mushrooms

2 tablespoons butter

3 tablespoons extra virgin olive oil

1 slice pancetta, diced

1 onion, minced

3 pounds veal breast chops,
cut through the bone into 3-inch pieces

Salt and freshly ground black pepper

Soak the mushrooms in a bowl of 2½ cups warm water for 30 minutes.

Melt the butter in the oil in a large casserole, preferably earthenware, over low heat. Add the pancetta and onion and, after 5 minutes, the veal pieces. Keeping the heat low, turn the veal every 5 minutes with a wooden spoon until the pieces begin to brown.

Drain the mushrooms, reserving the water. Season the veal with salt and pepper and add the mushrooms. Continue cooking over low heat for about 3 hours, turning the pieces frequently and adding some of the mushroom water whenever the liquid begins to dry out.

Serve this dish with Cornmeal Polenta (page 254).

CONTORNO

CONTORNO

PATATE AL TIMO
POTATOES BAKED WITH THYME

Serves four to six

2 pounds potatoes, peeled and cut into chunks

2 tablespoons extra virgin olive oil

Leaves from 1 sprig thyme, chopped

Salt and freshly ground black pepper

Preheat the oven to 350°F.

Place the potatoes in a large bowl; add the oil and thyme and toss to coat. Spread the potatoes out in a single layer on a baking sheet and bake for 1 hour, turning the pieces over after about 45 minutes. Season with salt and pepper and serve.

POLENTA DI MAIS
CORNMEAL POLENTA

Serves four to six

½ teaspoon salt

1 tablespoon extra virgin olive oil

2½ cups cornmeal

Fill a large saucepan with 8 cups water and add the salt. Place over medium heat and when it is just comes to a boil, add the oil, then pour the cornmeal in slowly, stirring continuously and always in the same direction to keep lumps from forming.

Continue cooking, stirring often, for 40 minutes; if the polenta starts to dry out, pour in a little boiling water. The polenta is ready when it is the consistency of soft mashed potatoes and comes off the sides of the saucepan easily.

Pour any leftover polenta onto a plate, cover with a dish towel, and store in the refrigerator. It can then be sliced and fried in vegetable oil.

FAGIOLI CANNELLINI ALL'UCCELLETTO
STEWED CANNELLINI BEANS

Serves six

3 tablespoons extra virgin olive oil

2 cloves garlic

1 sprig sage

4 cups cooked cannellini beans (see page 224)

Salt and freshly ground black pepper

¼ cup *passata* (page 86)

Heat the oil in an earthenware pot. Crush the garlic cloves with the flat side of a knife, peel them, and add them to the pot along with the sage. As soon as the garlic begins to color, add the beans and season with salt and pepper. Remove the garlic and sage.

Stir the beans until they start to look dry, then stir in the *passata*. Cook, covered, for 15 minutes more, adding a little water if the beans start to dry out. Serve piping hot.

INSALATA DI SONCINO ALL'ARANCIA
LAMB'S LETTUCE SALAD WITH ORANGE DRESSING

Serves four to six

½ pound lamb's lettuce (mâche) or other small salad leaves

4 teaspoons sesame seeds

2 tablespoons extra virgin olive oil

1 teaspoon balsamic vinegar

2 tablespoons freshly squeezed orange juice

Salt and freshly ground black pepper

Put the lamb's lettuce in a salad bowl.

Heat a small nonstick pan over medium-low heat, add the sesame seeds, and toast them for no more than a minute, stirring or shaking them constantly to keep them from burning. Transfer to a small plate to cool.

In a small bowl, whisk the oil with the vinegar and orange juice; season with salt and pepper. Toss the dressing with the lettuce and sprinkle with the sesame seeds.

CONTORNO

PURÉ DI CECI
CHICKPEA PUREE

Yields about four cups

1½ cups dried chickpeas

Baking soda

2 cloves garlic

1 sprig rosemary

Salt

Put the chickpeas in a large bowl of water and add a pinch of baking soda. Leave them to soak for 12 hours, then drain them and rinse well.

Crush the garlic cloves with the flat side of a knife.

In a large earthenware pot, combine the chickpeas with the garlic, rosemary, and a pinch of salt. Add water to cover. Bring to a boil, then reduce the heat and simmer for about 2 hours, until the chickpeas are soft, adding water as needed. Drain, remove the garlic, transfer to a food mill or food processor, and puree the chickpeas. Transfer the pureed chickpeas to a skillet and cook, stirring, to thicken and dry them out a little.

SECONDO

BACCALÀ FRITTO CON CONTORNO DI PURÉ DI CECI
FRIED SALT COD WITH CHICKPEA PUREE

Serves four

4 pieces salt cod, each weighing 7 ounces before soaking

5 tablespoons all-purpose flour

¼ cup extra virgin olive oil

Chickpea Puree (opposite)

Rosemary sprigs for garnish

The night before serving, immerse the cod in a large bowl of cold water to cover. Soak for 24 hours, changing the water several times. Drain the cod, then simmer in fresh water to cover for 10 minutes. Drain and pat dry. Dip the cod pieces in the flour and set aside.

Heat the oil in a skillet over medium heat; add the cod and sauté until the fish is browned, about 4 minutes per side.

Heat the chickpea puree. To serve, place a large spoonful of chickpea puree on each plate, and place the cod in the middle. Garnish with a sprig of rosemary.

I recommend using Icelandic cod whenever you can find it, and choose the thickest pieces for this recipe.

PANE

PANE CON I FICHI SECCHI E LE UVETTE
FIG AND RAISIN BREAD

Yields one large loaf

1 cup golden raisins

3 tablespoons sugar

1 cup cold black tea

1⅓ cups coarsely chopped dried figs

1 envelope (about 2¼ teaspoons) active dry yeast

2 cups all-purpose flour, plus more for dusting

2 cups bread flour

1 teaspoon salt

3 tablespoons butter, softened

1 egg

Soak the golden raisins in a bowl of warm water for 20 minutes; drain and pat dry. In a separate bowl, stir 1 tablespoon of the sugar into the tea until dissolved. Add the figs and soak them for 3 minutes; drain and pat dry.

Dissolve the yeast in ¼ cup warm water. Sift the two flours together into a bowl. Add the salt, yeast, the remaining 2 tablespoons sugar, the butter, egg, and enough room-temperature water to form a dough (about ¾ cup). Work the ingredients together until the dough is smooth and shiny, about 10 minutes.

Dip the golden raisins and figs in flour, then work them into the dough. Place the dough in a bowl, cover with a dish towel, and leave in a warm place to rise until doubled in size, about 1½ hours.

Press down on the dough and form it into a loaf about 10 inches long. Place on a baking sheet lined with parchment paper. Leave to rise for 1 hour.

Preheat the oven to 400°F.

Sprinkle the loaf with flour and bake for about 40 minutes, until the loaf is golden brown on top and sounds hollow when tapped on the bottom.

Though this is a sweet bread, it goes very well with cheese; it keeps well for about five days.

PANE BIANCO CASERECCIO
WHITE COUNTRY-STYLE BREAD

Yields one large loaf

1 envelope (about 2¼ teaspoons) active dry yeast

3 cups bread flour

1 teaspoon salt

4 cups all-purpose flour

The starter for this bread is very soft and best made in a mixer. The evening before baking, dissolve the yeast in ¾ cup lukewarm water. Add 2 cups of the bread flour and the salt, then work the ingredients into a smooth, soft dough. Place it in a bowl in a warm, dry place and cover with a dish towel. Leave it overnight; in the morning it should be at least twice the size.

Add the remaining 1 cup bread flour, the all-purpose flour, and 1¾ cups water and work it for about 10 minutes, until you have a smooth dough. Put it back in the bowl, cover with a dish towel, and set aside to rise until doubled in size again, about 1½ hours. Press down on the dough, turn it onto a floured surface, and knead it gently. Shape it into a loaf and place it on a parchment paper–lined baking sheet. Leave to rise for 30 minutes.

Preheat the oven to 425°F. Bake the bread for about 35 minutes, until the top is golden brown and the bottom sounds hollow when tapped.

There is always bread on the table during Tuscan meals. This recipe, with so little yeast, keeps longer than most. But even if it goes stale, bread is rarely thrown out. It can be used for making crumbs; toasted to serve with soup; and, in summer, turned into Panzanella (page 102).

BISCOTTI SALATI MAREMMANI
MAREMMAN SAVORY BISCOTTI

Makes about forty biscotti

2 envelopes (5 teaspoons) active dry yeast

12 cups all-purpose flour

1 cup white wine

2 cups extra virgin olive oil

1 teaspoon anise seeds

1 teaspoon salt

Preheat the oven to 400°F.

Dissolve the yeast in a bowl with ¼ cup warm water. Heap the flour on a work surface and form a well in the center. Carefully place all the ingredients, along with 1 cup water, in the well and work the flour gently into them.

When you have a workable dough, rub pieces between your hands to make long snake shapes, then cut each into 10-inch lengths. Twist them around to form pretzel shapes.

Bring a large pot of salted water to a boil. Drop the biscotti carefully into the water a few at a time. When they float to the surface, remove them with a slotted spoon. Dry them on a dish towel, then place them on baking sheets. Place in the oven and bake 15 to 20 minutes, until they are golden.

For a spicier biscotti, add some chili to the dough. These biscotti will keep well in an airtight container for up to three weeks. We eat them as a snack.

PALLINE DI DATTERI E COCCO
DATE AND COCONUT BALLS

Yields about thirty-five balls

½ cup (1 stick) butter

1 egg

2 cups pitted dates, finely chopped

½ pound sweet, dry cookies (such as vanilla wafers), crushed

Grated meat of 1 coconut

Melt the butter in a large saucepan over low heat. Remove from the heat, cool slightly, then beat in the egg and add the dates. Return the saucepan to the stovetop over low heat and stir until the ingredients are blended. Remove from the heat and add the crushed cookies.

Shape the mixture into about 35 small balls and roll them in coconut. Place them on a tray and refrigerate for 5 hours. Roll them in coconut again before serving.

Dried figs can be used instead of dates.

FRUTTA SECCA RIPIENA
STUFFED DRIED FRUIT

Yields forty-eight pieces

12 dried apricots

12 dates

12 dried figs

12 prunes

1 egg white

2 cups confectioners' sugar

1¼ cups finely chopped hazelnuts

7 ounces dark chocolate, chopped

If the fruit is very hard, soak for a few minutes in hot water (each in a separate bowl). Drain the fruit, dry well, and set aside for 1 hour.

In a bowl, beat the egg white until stiff peaks form, then fold in the confectioners' sugar and the hazelnuts.

Open up the apricots, dates, figs, and prunes by carefully cutting them lengthwise. Remove the pits from the prunes and dates. Stuff the egg and hazelnut mixture inside the fruits and squeeze them back into their natural shapes. Refrigerate for 1 hour.

Melt the chocolate in a double boiler or in a heatproof bowl placed over simmering water. Dunk each piece of fruit halfway into the melted chocolate. Stand them on a parchment paper–lined baking sheet and set aside until the chocolate sets.

Store in an airtight container in a cool place; they will keep for up to two weeks. Serve after dinner with coffee for a different type of dessert.

TARTUFI
TRUFFLES

Yields about thirty-five balls

1 cup heavy cream

1 pound dark chocolate, grated

Cocoa powder for rolling

Grated coconut for rolling

Finely chopped toasted hazelnuts for rolling

In a medium saucepan, bring the cream just to a boil; remove from the heat. Add the chocolate and stir until it is completely melted. Transfer to a bowl, cover, and refrigerate for a couple of hours to cool completely.

Shape the mixture into about 35 little balls and roll them in cocoa powder, coconut, and/or hazelnuts.

For a spicy version, add chili powder to the chocolate and cream.

SALAME DI CIOCCOLATA
CHOCOLATE SALAMI

Serves eight to ten

2 eggs

½ cup (1 stick) butter, melted

½ cup granulated sugar

1 cup cocoa powder

7 ounces sweet, dry cookies (such as vanilla wafers), crushed

½ cup confectioners' sugar

In a large bowl, beat the eggs with the butter, granulated sugar, and cocoa powder. Stir in the crushed cookies.

Butter a sheet of parchment paper thoroughly. Form the mixture into a salami shape in the middle of the paper, then wrap the edges of the paper around it well. Refrigerate for a few hours, then roll the salami in the confectioners' sugar. Slice and serve.

When my son Corso was going to boarding school, he would always take back lots of this salami to share with his friends.

DOLCE

TORTA DI ARANCE
ORANGE CAKE

Serves eight

For the cake

1¼ cups all-purpose flour

1 tablespoon baking powder

½ cup (1 stick) butter, softened

⅔ cup sugar

2 eggs

½ cup milk

Grated zest of 3 lemons

For the syrup

Juice of 5 oranges

½ cup sugar

For the filling

One 8-ounce jar orange marmalade

3 oranges, peeled and thinly sliced

Preheat the oven to 350°F and line a high-sided 9-inch round cake pan with parchment paper.

Beat all the cake ingredients together in a mixer or food processor, then pour the mixture into the prepared cake pan. Bake for about 35 minutes, until a toothpick or skewer stuck into the center of the cake comes out clean. Invert the cake onto a rack to cool.

To make the syrup, combine the orange juice and sugar and stir until the sugar dissolves.

When the cake has cooled, use a serrated knife to cut it through the middle horizontally. Pour half the syrup over the bottom part and spread marmalade over it. Replace the top half of the cake, spread a thin layer of marmalade over it, arrange the orange slices on top, and drizzle with the remaining syrup.

268

DOLCE

CROSTATA DI PERE ALLA CREMA
PEAR AND CUSTARD TART

Serves eight

For the pastry

¾ cup all-purpose flour

¾ cup semolina flour

½ cup confectioners' sugar

⅓ cup cocoa powder

Salt

2 egg yolks

½ cup (1 stick) butter, softened

For the filling

4 tablespoons sugar

1 pound pears, peeled, cored, and sliced

⅓ cup finely chopped almonds

1 egg, separated

1 cup milk

Place both kinds of flour, the confectioners' sugar, cocoa powder, and a pinch of salt in the bowl of a mixer and mix to combine. Add the egg yolks and butter and beat on high speed for 30 seconds to make a smooth paste; don't allow the mixture to warm up. Shape the mixture into a ball, cover it with plastic wrap, and refrigerate for 1 hour.

Preheat the oven to 350°F and line a 9-inch round baking pan with parchment paper.

Thinly roll out the pastry and line the prepared pan with it.

Sprinkle 2 tablespoons sugar over the bottom of the pastry case. Arrange the pear slices over the sugar and sprinkle with the almonds.

In a bowl, beat the remaining 2 tablespoons sugar into the egg yolk and add the milk. Beat the egg white until stiff peaks form, then fold it into the yolk mixture and pour it over the pears. Place in the oven and bake for about 40 minutes, until the crust is lightly browned and the center is golden.

270

DOLCE

TORTA DI MELE ANTICA
OLD-FASHIONED APPLE CAKE

Serves eight

1 cup golden raisins

1 cup all-purpose flour,
plus more for dusting the raisins

1 tablespoon baking powder

½ cup (1 stick) butter, softened

¾ cup sugar

3 eggs

½ cup milk

Grated zest of 1 lemon

⅓ cup pine nuts

5 baking apples (such as Golden Delicious),
peeled, cored, and thinly sliced

Soak the golden raisins in a bowl of hot water for
1 hour. Drain, dry, and dust them in flour.

Preheat the oven to 400°F and line a high-sided
9-inch cake pan with parchment paper.

In a mixer, cream the butter and sugar, then add
the 1 cup flour, baking powder, eggs, milk, and
lemon zest and beat for 3 minutes. Add the pine
nuts and golden raisins.

Pour the mixture into the prepared baking pan
and spread the apple slices over the top. Bake
for about 45 minutes, until the top is golden,
then invert the cake onto a rack to cool.

DOLCE

CUBI DI CAPRESE
CAPRI CUBES

Yields about twelve cubes

1 cup (2 sticks) butter, softened

¾ cup granulated sugar

5 ounces dark chocolate, finely chopped

1¾ cups almonds, finely chopped

5 eggs, separated

2 tablespoons confectioners' sugar

Preheat the oven to 400°F and line an 11-inch rectangular baking pan with parchment paper.

In a bowl, cream the butter with half of the granulated sugar. Add the chocolate and almonds.

In a separate bowl, beat the egg yolks with the remaining granulated sugar and add to the chocolate mixture. Beat the egg whites until stiff peaks form and fold them into the mixture.

Pour into the prepared baking pan and bake for about 35 minutes, until the top is firm, then invert the cake onto a rack to cool. Cut the cake into 2-inch cubes and sprinkle them with confectioners' sugar.

DOLCE

SORBETTO AL MANDARINO
MANDARIN SORBET

Serves six

12 mandarin oranges

¾ cup sugar

1 lemon

1 egg white

Grate the zest from 2 of the mandarin oranges. Place the zest in a saucepan with the sugar and ½ cup water. Bring to a boil, then reduce the heat and simmer for 10 minutes. Juice all the mandarins (to yield about 2 cups juice) and the lemon, and add all the juice to the saucepan. Strain the mixture and refrigerate until cold. Transfer to an ice cream maker and churn according to the manufacturer's instructions.

While the sorbet is churning, beat the egg white until stiff peaks form, and work it into the sorbet a few minutes before you remove it from the ice cream maker. (You may not need to use all of the egg white; taste the mixture and use your judgment.)

If you don't have an ice cream maker, place the sorbet mixture—without the egg white— in a bowl and freeze for at least four hours, stirring once every hour. When you stir it for the last time, fold in the beaten egg white. Store the sorbet in a sealed container in the freezer. If it freezes too hard to serve, blend it for a few seconds on high speed.

TORTA DI MELE CARAMELLATA
CARAMELIZED APPLE TART

Serves six

For the pastry

3 eggs

2 cups all-purpose flour

½ cup sugar

Grated zest of 1 lemon

10 tablespoons (1 stick plus 2 tablespoons) butter, chilled and cut into pieces

For the filling

5 crisp apples (such as Golden Delicious), peeled, cored, and quartered

4 tablespoons (½ stick) butter

⅔ cup sugar

Greek yogurt for serving (optional)

To make the pastry, boil the eggs in a pot of water for 7 minutes. Drain, cool, then peel them and separate the yolks from the whites. Save the whites for another use.

Place the flour and sugar in a food processor; add the lemon zest, butter, and boiled egg yolks, and process until the dough comes together. Place the dough between two sheets of parchment paper and roll it out about ⅛ inch thick and large enough to line the bottom of a 11-inch round tart pan. Refrigerate for 1 hour.

Preheat the oven to 375°F and line a 9-inch round pie pan with parchment paper.

To make the filling, in a saucepan, combine the apple quarters with the butter and sugar. Place over medium heat and cook, covered, for about 5 minutes, until softened. Remove the cover, turn the heat up, and continue cooking until the sugar caramelizes.

Spread the caramelized apples in an artful formation on the prepared pie pan and set aside to cool. Remove the dough from the refrigerator, place it on top of the apples, press down around the edges to seal them, and bake for about 35 minutes, until the surface of the pie is golden.

Remove the pie from the oven, place on a wire rack to cool, then invert onto a plate. Remove the parchment paper and serve with Greek yogurt, if using.

BRIOCHES E CORNETTI
BREAKFAST PASTRIES

Yields about twelve pastries

1¼ cups milk

1 envelope (2¼ teaspoons) active dry yeast

3½ cups all-purpose flour

1 cup sugar

3 egg yolks

¾ cup (1½ sticks) butter, softened

Grated zest of ½ lemon

½ teaspoon salt

Apricot or raspberry jam (for *cornetti*)

½ cup golden raisins (for braids)

Sugar for sprinkling (for brioches)

In a saucepan, warm ½ cup of the milk until lukewarm. In a large bowl, dissolve the yeast in the lukewarm milk. Add the flour, sugar, 2 of the egg yolks, the butter, lemon zest, salt, and the rest of the milk, and with a wooden spoon work the ingredients together well to form a smooth dough. Turn the dough out onto a workspace and knead for 5 minutes. Place the dough in a bowl, cover it with plastic wrap or a dish towel, and leave it to rise until it has doubled in size, about 2 hours. Shape it in one of the following ways:

Cornetti: Roll the dough out to about a ⅛ inch thickness, and cut triangles with a narrow base and long sides. Place a heaping teaspoonful jam in the center of each triangle, then begin rolling the triangles from the short side, ending with the point. Bend the thin ends gently into a crescent shape.

Braids: Soak the golden raisins in warm water for 10 minutes, then dry them and mix them into the dough. Take 3 small pieces of dough, roll them between your hands to form sausage shapes, then braid them together, pressing down well at each end to keep the pieces together.

Brioches: Break off a piece of dough the size of a small potato and shape it into a ball, then sit it on a baking sheet and lightly press down on it. Take another slightly smaller piece, roll it into a ball, and place it on top. Sprinkle with a few grains of sugar.

Place the dough shapes on a baking sheet lined with parchment paper and leave them to rise until doubled in size (about an hour).

Preheat the oven to 400°F. Brush the dough shapes with the remaining egg yolk and bake for about 25 minutes. When they're done, the tops will be shiny and golden—and your whole house will be filled with the wonderful smell of fresh pastries.

These dough shapes can be frozen and baked at another time. Make the shapes and put them in the freezer after the first rise. Remove them from the freezer in the evening to defrost and rise overnight. The next morning, brush with beaten egg yolk and bake according to the recipe.

CONVERSION CHART

LIQUID CONVERSIONS

U.S.	Metric
1 tsp	5 ml
1 tbs	15 ml
2 tbs	30 ml
3 tbs	45 ml
¼ cup	60 ml
⅓ cup	75 ml
⅓ cup + 1 tbs	90 ml
⅓ cup + 2 tbs	100 ml
½ cup	120 ml
⅔ cup	150 ml
¾ cup	180 ml
¾ cup + 2 tbs	200 ml
1 cup	240 ml
1 cup + 2 tbs	275 ml
1 ¼ cups	300 ml
1 ⅓ cups	325 ml
1 ½ cups	350 ml
1 ⅔ cups	375 ml
1 ¾ cups	400 ml
1 ¾ cups + 2 tbs	450 ml
2 cups (1 pint)	475 ml
2 ½ cups	600 ml
3 cups	720 ml
4 cups (1 quart)	945 ml (1,000 ml is 1 liter)

WEIGHT CONVERSIONS

U.S./U.K.	Metric
½ oz	14 g
1 oz	28 g
1 ½ oz	43 g
2 oz	57 g
2 ½ oz	71 g
3 oz	85 g
3 ½ oz	100 g
4 oz	113 g
5 oz	142 g
6 oz	170 g
7 oz	200 g
8 oz	227 g
9 oz	255 g
10 oz	284 g
11 oz	312 g
12 oz	340 g
13 oz	368 g
14 oz	400 g
15 oz	425 g
1 lb	454 g

OVEN TEMPERATURES

°F	Gas Mark	°C
250	1/2	120
275	1	140
300	2	150
325	3	165
350	4	180
375	5	190
400	6	200
425	7	220
450	8	230
475	9	240
500	10	260
550	Broil	290

All conversions are approximate.

INDEX

(Page references in *italic* refer to illustrations.)

A

Acciughe Fritte, 96, *97*
Acciughe sotto Pesto, 94, *95*
Acquacotta, 228, *229*
Agnello al Latte, 46, *47*
Alici Fresche con l'Uva, 158, *159*
almond(s):
    Biscotti, 190
    Capri Cubes, 272
    Cookies, Peaches with, 138, *139*
    Cornmeal Cake, 64, *65*
Amor Polenta, 64, *65*
anchovy(ies):
    and Bell Pepper Toast, 82, *83*
    Fresh, with Grapes, 158, *159*
    Fried, 96, *97*
    in Olive Oil, 94, *95*
antipasti (starters), 13. *See also* focaccia
    Anchovies, Fresh, with Grapes,
        158, *159*
    Anchovies, Fried, 96, *97*
    Anchovies in Olive Oil, 94, *95*
    Artichokes, Stuffed, 20, *21*
    Arugula Salad with Pomegranate,
        222, *223*
    Asparagus Chicory Salad, 226
    Asparagus with Pancetta, 22
    Autumn Salad, 148, *149*
    Beef, Cured, with Herbs, 114, *115*
    Bell Pepper and Anchovy Toast,
        82, *83*
    Bell Pepper and Sun-Dried Tomato
        Tartlets, 76, *77*
    Cannellini Beans and Black Kale on
        Toast, 224, *225*
    Cheese, Fresh, *23*, 24, *25*
    Chicken Liver on Toast, 154, *155*
    Chicory Pie, 28, *29*
    Eggplant and Peppers, Sweet and
        Sour, 90
    Eggplant Baked with Cheese, 88
    Eggplant Mille-Feuille, 86, *87*
    Eggplant with Mint and Yogurt, 88
    Fava Bean and Artichoke Salad,
        22, *23*

Leek Flan, 26, *27*
Lettuce Tart, 80, *81*
Orange and Black Olive Salad, 226
Paté, Homemade, 152
Pears, Caramelized, with Robiola
    Cheese, 220, *221*
Pizza, 212, *213*
Prunes Wrapped in Pancetta, 188
Radicchio and Walnut Salad,
    156, *157*
Rolls, Filled, 153
Spinach Pies, Individual, 150, *151*
Summer Salad, 92, *93*
Zucchini, Stuffed, 91
Zucchini, Sweet and Sour Fried,
    84, *85*
Zucchini Flowers, Fried, 78
apple(s):
    Cake, Old-Fashioned, 270, *271*
    Caramelized, Tart, 276, *277*
    Pork Braised with, 185
    Strudel, Grandma's, 67
apricots, in Stuffed Dried Fruit,
    262, *263*
Arista con Ripieno di Prugne, 240, *241*
Arrosto di Vitello con Salsa alle Noci,
    188, *189*
artichoke(s):
    bottling, 18
    Carbonara Pasta with Fava Beans and,
        40
    and Fava Bean Salad, 22, *23*
    Fricasseed, 48
    Omelette, 48, *49*
    Pan-Cooked, 44, *45*
    Pan-Cooked Spring Vegetables,
        52, *53*
    Stuffed, 20, *21*
    Vicarello Soup, 32, *33*
Arugula Salad with Pomegranate,
    222, *223*
Asparagi Saltati, 22
asparagus:
    with Pancetta, 22
    Pan-Cooked Spring Vegetables,
        52, *53*
    Risotto, 34

Asparagus Chicory Salad, 226
Autumn Salad, 148, *149*

B

*Baccalà Fritto con Contorno di Purè
    di Ceci*, 256, *257*
bacon, 11. *See also* Pancetta
Barbecue Seasoning, 180
Basil Pesto, 100
Bavarese di Yogurt con Pesche e Lime,
    132, *133*
Bavarian Cream, Yogurt, with Peaches
    and Lime, 132, *133*
beans. *See also* cannellini bean(s);
    fava bean(s)
        Chickpea Puree, 256
beef:
    brisket, in Mixed Braised Meats,
        182, *183*
    Cured, with Herbs, 114, *115*
Beer-Baked Veal Shank, 174, *175*
Biscotti, Almond, 190
Biscotti alle Nocciole, 198, *199*
Biscotti Salati Maremmani, 260, *261*
Biscotti, Maremman Savory, 260, *261*
Boar, Wild, Stew, 242, *243*
Bocconcini di Agnello, 54
Bowls, Whole-Wheat Pastry, *231*, 232
bread. *See also* focaccia; toast
    Fig and Raisin, 258, *259*
    Filled Rolls, 153
    Honey Rolls, 208, *209*
    Pizza, 212, *213*
    Salad, Tuscan, 102, *103*
    White Country-Style, 260
breadsticks, turning extra dough into,
    26
breakfast:
    Honey Rolls, 208, *209*
    Pastries, 278, *279*
Bream with Wild Fennel, 58, *59*
Brioche Dove, 68, *69*
Brioches, 278, *279*
Brodo di Carne, 164
Brodo Vegetale, 222
Broth with Egg, 164, *165*
Budino di Riso, 206, *207*